THE UNIQUE GRIEF OF
SUICIDE

Questions and Hope

TOM SMITH

iUniverse, Inc.
Bloomington

The Unique Grief of Suicide
Questions and Hope

Copyright © 2013 Tom Smith

iUniverse books may be ordered through booksellers or by contacting:

iUniverse
1663 Liberty Drive
Bloomington, IN 47403
www.iuniverse.com
1-800-Authors (1-800-288-4677)

ISBN: 978-1-4759-7003-6 (sc)
ISBN: 978-1-4759-7005-0 (hc)
ISBN: 978-1-4759-7004-3 (e)

Library of Congress Control Number: 2013900051

Printed in the United States of America

iUniverse rev. date: 2/27/2013

DEDICATION

To Karla, who graced our life for twenty-six years

Contents

Foreword

Tom Smith's book *The Unique Grief of Suicide* is an excellent guide to what to expect as one journeys the path of grief due to a completed suicide.

Suicide is rooted in a brain disorder. Society does not view this mental illness in the same way that it views heart disease or diabetes. A mental illness is an illness just like cancer or heart disease, but it attacks a different part of the human body. People do not suffer from mental illness because they want to, but because they have been afflicted with a brain disorder. Misconceptions about mental illness bring shame or embarrassment to the person with the illness as well as to family members.

People who complete suicide die as a result of this illness. It is helpful for survivors of a suicide to view the death as resulting from an illness. There is no reason for survivors to feel embarrassed or ashamed. *The Unique Grief of Suicide* articulates this fact well.

Survivors can perform a great service to society by educating people about mental illness and suicide. The statistics included herein clearly address the prevalence of this disease in society.

There are over thirty-five thousand completed suicides in our country each year. The vast majority of these suicides occur as a result of some form of mental illness.

The grief journey is a long and life-altering process, one that never completely goes away. Tom Smith discusses the various holidays that are especially painful for survivors. The obvious holidays, such as Thanksgiving or Christmas, are difficult, but also days like Valentine's Day or Mother's Day or Father's Day are also extremely painful, depending on the relationship that was lost. This book provides helpful ways to commemorate these painful times.

The Unique Grief of Suicide provides clear direction to anyone who lost a loved one from suicide. It is concise and to the point. This journey is perilous, but Smith outlines the path and points the reader to the goal of assimilation. Each person finds unique ways to make this journey. This book clearly and effectively guides a suicide griever to a grief that is more manageable and a life that is not dominated by the suicide.

Rev. Charles T. Rubey
Founder and Director of LOSS (Loving Outreach to Survivors of Suicide)
Administration, Program Development
crubey@catholiccharities.net

Catholic Charities of the Archdiocese of Chicago
721 North LaSalle Street
Chicago, IL 60654
Office: (312) 655-7280
Fax: (312) 655-0219
www.catholiccharities.net

Introduction

Suicide shouts questions and demands answers. But often the answers don't come.

The purpose of *The Unique Grief of Suicide* is to ask those questions, respond to them as best we can, and help us live in peace with the questions that evade answers. For those of us who have lost a loved one to suicide, achieving that purpose can be difficult, painful, seemingly unattainable, and at best a gradual, unpredictable process with no absolute end. But that process is also rewarding, comforting, and ultimately satisfying. Asking the questions honestly and courageously gives us the best chance for coping with the grief that follows a suicide.

The Unique Grief of Suicide is intended primarily for people who grieve the death of a loved one to suicide. This focus is not limited to people who just recently experienced a suicide. People who are many years removed from that tragic loss and who think "that is all behind me" will also find this book helpful because some areas of this unique grief are often left unresolved, and the perspective of years and the reflection this book provides can lead to fuller resolution.

For other people, their reaction to a suicide is so wrenching that they quickly try to end the grief by walling it off within themselves, stuffing it in a remote corner of their psyche in the belief that they can't or won't deal with it any more. For some men, that is the "manly" thing to do—bury it, and get on with life. For other men and women, it's a matter of time and energy: "I don't have the time or energy to deal with my suicide grief right now, so I will get by this as quickly as possible and do what I have to do with the other parts of my life." Years later, the suicide still haunts them periodically, even though they don't want or know how to cope with it; so they continue to neglect their slow-burning and ongoing grief.

Other people experienced the suicide of a parent, sibling, or friend when they were children or adolescents, and they were not old enough or mature enough to process the grief sufficiently. As adults, they may need to go back to that suicide, ask different or even the same questions from an older perspective, and revisit the suicide in order to experience greater peace in the present.

The Unique Grief of Suicide is intended for all these categories of people. And, as the statistics in the book will show, that is a lot of potential readers. But there are more:

- psychiatrists and counselors
- pastors and social workers
- funeral directors and coroners
- coworkers, friends, and neighbors

All of these personal friends and professionals can benefit from these few pages as they seek to understand and provide comfort to people who grieve a suicide.

Many questions follow a suicide. Some of these questions are critical and fundamental; they require comments and sincere attempts to answer them. But some emerge from ignorance, stigma, and myth and need to be dismissed in order to leave the focus on more basic questions. There is no such thing as a *bad* question. But questions that stem from myth need to be analyzed in order to be eliminated. Successful suicide grief needs to concentrate on the genuine issues.

Myths about Suicide

1. One myth about suicide says, "Suicide is for cowards." Put another way, "Suicide is the easy way out." It takes a lot of strength, determination, and even courage for people to kill themselves. The innate desire to preserve our own life is so powerful that overcoming that desire demands an extraordinary amount of willpower and even practice to complete a suicide. There are many more suicide attempts than there are completions. Those multiple attempts point to some desire to die but also indicate how difficult it is to actually complete the act. Questions that arise from this myth must be acknowledged, but it is best to dismiss them quickly and move on to other more substantive questions.

2. Another myth says, "Suicide is selfish." To quote Dr. Thomas Joiner in his book *Myths about Suicide*, "There is scant evidence that those who die by suicide are more selfish than others. On the other hand, there is abundant evidence that, far from being selfish, suicide decedents (incorrectly) believe their deaths will be a blessing to others."[1] Once again, if someone grieving the loss of a loved one by suicide hears or thinks about the "selfishness" of the death, it is best to discard that notion as soon as possible, since this thought will overly complicate and delay the grieving process.

---

1   Joiner, *Myths about Suicide*, 44.

3. There is also the misconception that people who die by suicide don't make plans beyond their deaths. Evidence shows over and over again that people who complete suicide do make plans beyond their deaths even while they plan those deaths. They are ambivalent about killing themselves, and are aware that they may not be able to do it when the time and occasion present themselves. These plans are contradictory from one point of view, but they are consistent with the evidence that suicide is extremely difficult. Grievers should not spend time and emotional energy on this issue.[2]

4. It appears that sometimes people take their own lives "on a whim." This myth is quite entrenched and appears in works of fiction, movies, and newspaper accounts of suicides. But close analysis undermines this common misrepresentation. If it were true, there would be millions more suicides each year as people see opportunities to jump from a bridge, use a gun or knife on themselves, see a train approaching, or open a medicine cabinet. There is more to a completed suicide than a whim or spontaneous impulse. It seems more likely that people think about suicide previously, perhaps even file away plans in their brains, and seize a moment when it presents itself to act on the plan. Alcohol or drugs may also be involved. While this misconception is more deeply embedded in our society than some of the other myths, and is promoted by some celebrities and professionals, it seems more helpful to grievers to follow the research of Dr. Joiner, Dr. Kimberly Van Orden, and others who propose a different view of why people take their own lives.[3]

5. Finally, there is the myth that only certain types of people die by suicide: people who are poor, look disheveled, or have an obvious mental illness. The facts are that suicides occur within

---

2   Ibid., 62ff.
3   See chapter 5.

every stratum and economic level of society. Suicide happens in every country, century, culture, and climate. Furthermore, many mental illnesses are not obvious. Appearances don't matter. Do not let appearances or the question "How could this happen within our family?" interfere with the core *grief work* that needs greater attention.[4] Coping with grief successfully is work that requires intense emotional focus; the ability to identify and separate related but different feelings; the courage to find ways to manage the negative emotions; and thinking clearly when unaccustomed, powerful feelings dominate our thoughts. Getting through this personal work is time-consuming, demanding, and draining and often requires assistance from other people, both professionals and personal friends and family. Suicide intensifies this process. Grief is work.

These misconceptions about suicide indicate some of the unique complications of suicide grief. They must be addressed if they emerge as parts of the aftermath of a suicide. But one suggestion in this book is to spend more time, thought, and emotional energy on more basic questions. These are the questions that form the structure of this book. There are five of them: *Who, What, When, Where,* and *Why.* I have devoted an entire chapter to each of these questions.

Throughout *The Unique Grief of Suicide* I refer to my own experience with the suicide of my daughter, Karla. I make these references to illustrate aspects of suicide grief, not as a memoir. Suicide grief is extremely personal, and sharing our individual stories of struggle and comfort is one way for us to cope with our grief. "You are not alone" is a powerful message for suicide grievers.

---

4   See http://www.nimh.nih.gov/health/publications/suicide-in-the-us-statistics-and-prevention/index.shtml for more details.

Some questions raised by a suicide may not be totally answerable. The mysteries of life and death, especially death by suicide, are not easily categorized into a convenient question-and-answer formula. Not everything in life and death is a problem to be solved or a question to be answered. Mystery remains. And when faced with the mysteries of life and death, it is better to wonder at the mystery and accept that some things in life and death are simply not explainable. Different people have different thresholds of mystery, but most of us admit that some life experiences remain at least ambiguous and ultimately beyond our comprehension. Suicide and suicide grief fit this experience of mystery.

This book acknowledges this mystery even as it asks questions and seeks answers to suicide and suicide grief. There is no contradiction between admitting the mystery and seeking some answers. It is important to know where the mystery begins and ends, and what is knowable. That's why a guide through suicide grief is so helpful. The experience is so complex that sorting through the complexities is a value in itself. Sorting through them is what this book tries to do, while accepting that some mystery will remain.

The ultimate goal of suicide grief work is assimilation. To assimilate a suicide into life is to absorb the pain and to incorporate the death into other aspects of life. The loss remains, but it is surrounded by other experiences, both memories of the past and the ongoing integration of new happenings in life. The suicide grief no longer dominates the rest of life. But the path to this goal of assimilation must go through the forest of thorny, frustrating, and painful questions raised by a suicide.

Each chapter ends with a short message on hope. Grieving a suicide can seem totally overwhelming and endless. The hope message insists that with time and enlightened grief work, anyone can get through the worst of the loss and eventually experience a satisfying life. That is the hope. It is both real and realistic.

The questions at the end of each chapter are intended for personal reflection or for sharing the responses with other people. This sharing could be in a support group.[5] But the sharing could also be within the family or with a friend. Two or more people could read a chapter and then respond to the questions together, face-to-face, on the phone, or online. This guided approach through a grief process has been helpful to many grievers. You can read *The Unique Grief of Suicide* alone, and you can move at the pace you choose. But you also might have a more successful grief journey if you do it with at least one other person.

In any case, I hope this approach of raising core questions about the *Who*, *What*, *When*, *Where*, and *Why* of suicide will lead you to assimilation and to some peace despite the devastating suicide of a loved one.

---

5   See www.KarlaSmithFoundation.org for more information on joining or starting a support group.

CHAPTER 1

Those Who Died and Those They Left Behind

THE *WHO* QUESTION

Of the nearly one million suicides worldwide during 2003, including the 31,484 in the United States, the 476 in Oklahoma, and the seventy in Tulsa, the suicide of my daughter, Karla, is the one tragedy that ripped apart my heart and my life. She was twenty-six at the time, seven years after the first onslaught of her bipolar disorder. Even though she had three years of mental stability between the beginning of her illness and her death by mental illness, she ended her desperate pain on Monday, January 13. Simultaneously, she slammed us into the swirling world of suicide survivor grief. In 2003, there were literally a million similar experiences. And 2003 happens every year.

Karla fit a high-risk profile for suicide. She had bipolar disorder, had attempted suicide three times previously, and was released three days earlier from a behavioral health care center where she spent ten days being treated for depression. All of those conditions increase the possibility of suicide. A week before she entered the center, she told us how worthless she thought she was; how much of a burden she was, not only on us but on the universe; and how she couldn't stop thinking of killing herself.

When the policeman came to our door in Shiloh, Illinois, and told us that the Tulsa police department informed him that "Karla Smith has died," it was devastating. He had no details on how she died, but I knew immediately that she took her own life. It was an overwhelming shock, but it was not a surprise. It is clearly the worst thing that has ever happened to me.

Karla

Karla is a twin, born, along with her brother, Kevin, on August 7, 1976, in Ottumwa, Iowa. They are our only children, and Fran and I have enjoyed being their parents. When they were two years old, we moved to Broken Arrow, Oklahoma, a middle-class suburb of Tulsa. Their childhood and adolescence were normal enough, and they both did well in school and socially.

Since infancy, Karla was adventuresome, curious, and attracted to performing arts: acting, dancing, speech, and drama. In high school, she was a star performer in school plays, a successful member of the speech team, winning state honors in a variety of categories. She also was elected treasurer of the school's student council, which had to do more with her popularity and an appealing campaign ("Karla's the Key") than with her money management skills.

Kevin's interests and personality developed in very different directions. While he too excelled in the classroom, with a special ability in math, his extracurricular energy focused on sports. He played basketball until his sophomore year and then focused on tennis, earning All-Conference Player of the Year honors his senior year, when his team placed second in state.

Predictably, they had different groups of friends, but it was a delight for us to get to know their friends as they progressed through high school. There were some typical adolescent issues we had to deal with, but it was generally a good time in the busy Smith household during those years. Despite their differences, Kevin and Karla remained their own best friends.

They chose different colleges; Kevin went to St. Louis University, and Karla to Incarnate Word in San Antonio. She transferred to Oklahoma State University in Stillwater, Oklahoma, for her sophomore year, primarily because she wanted to spend a year in a European student exchange program, and in order to expand the number of courses available to her in her major study area, English literature. She loved learning and was a bright, enthusiastic student (although she had trouble learning Latin and Spanish, and math was always a problem, mainly because she didn't see the point), and an active member of various clubs, including the poetry group and Amnesty International.

But we were not prepared for the beginning of the second semester of her sophomore year (1996), when she suddenly became seriously depressed. We were grateful that one of her favorite professors called us to say that she had dropped out of everything. She came home, and we got her a counselor and a psychiatrist who prescribed for her the first of many antidepressants. She attempted suicide during this period, but eventually she did well enough to attend the fall semester in Utrecht, the Netherlands, where she once again became depressed. She came home without completing any classes and ended up in a treatment center in Tulsa.

Her mania emerged in 1998, which was followed in 1999 with three years of stability, when she returned to Oklahoma State

University. She was three classes away from graduating with a 4.0 GPA when, unknown to us, she took herself off her lithium. Five months later she was in a major, extended manic phase that led to psychotic thinking and behavior. By Thanksgiving of 2002, she was back on her meds but moving into another depression. On New Year's Eve, 2002, Fran took her, in a catatonic state and with a suicide note in hand, to the Tulsa Behavioral Health Center, where she stayed for ten days. They released her on a Friday, against our wishes, and she shot herself the following Monday. She lives in our hearts but not in our lives.

The story of her life and our attempts to cope with her illness and death can be found in my previous book, *The Tattered Tapestry: A Family's Search for Peace with Bipolar Disorder.*[6]

A Few More Statistics

Karla is much more than a statistic. But she is also a statistic. And the numbers are significant as we try to understand and cope with the reality of so many people taking their own lives. The figures show us trends and suggest a profile of who is vulnerable to suicide. We may then create strategies to intervene and prevent future premature deaths.

There are many mysteries surrounding self-inflicted death: Why? What could I have done to prevent it? Who's to blame? And back again to why did the person do it? While the statistics don't solve the mysteries, the numbers do provide a context for trying to understand who those who complete suicides are and why they take their own lives. We need this general context as we address the puzzling and heart-wrenching questions generated by a suicide.

---

6   Published by iUniverse, 2005.

Officially, there were 38,364 reported suicides in the United States in 2010, the most recent figures that are available as I write this book. This number means that there is a suicide about every fourteen minutes, and a suicide attempt about every minute.[7] That is a huge number! Most of us were not aware of this epidemic until we experienced it personally, and even then many of us thought that our loved one was an unfortunate part of a smaller number. Knowing that there are so many suicides can be both comforting and discouraging. In terms of our personal grief, it does suggest that, along with the question of why did our loved one die by suicide, there is another question: Why do all these people take their lives?

Almost four males complete suicide for every female. Women, however, attempt suicide three times more often than men. The obvious conclusion is that men are much more successful at taking their lives, which means that fewer suicidal men get a second chance to stay alive. The difference between men and women in their suicide rate is significant information for suicide prevention efforts. On the other hand, once a person attempts suicide, whether male or female, the likelihood that this person will attempt it again increases. It may be that women make several attempts at suicide before they are successful while men complete the suicide in the first attempt. How does your loved one fit this profile? Is that knowledge comforting or discouraging?

The most common method for completing suicide is firearms. More than half of the people who die by suicide use this method. Men use it more often than women while the women use pills as their most common method. The greater use of firearms by men may account for their higher success rate on the first attempt. Karla's three unsuccessful attempts were all overdoses

---

7   American Foundation for Suicide Prevention, http://www.afsp.org/index. cfm?fuseaction=home.viewPage&page_id=050FEA9F-B064-4092-B1135C3A70DE1FDA.

of prescription pills but her final, successful attempt was with a firearm. Did she avoid the method of overdose this last time because she wasn't successful the previous times? Did she seek another method that would be more definite in its outcome? Or did she simply find the hidden rifle and decide then to use it? All these remain unanswered questions.

Whether the suicide of your loved one fits the statistical profile or not, how does the method of death impact you? Does it really matter to you how they died? For many survivors, it does seem to make a difference. Our concern is that we didn't want them to suffer physically too much. Their emotional pain was excruciating enough. My wish for Karla was that she would use a method that would not be immediately fatal, and give her another chance to reconsider. The rifle all but took away that option. Reality, of course, destroyed my wish and became another part of my suicide grief.

Suicide rates are lowest among people who are married when compared to people who are divorced, separated, or widowed. That makes sense probably because married people have someone to talk with as well as someone who can monitor a potential suicide and try to keep the person safe. It may be too that people who are divorced, separated, or widowed more likely live alone after they had the experience of living with others. That lifestyle change may contribute to a depression that may lead to suicide. Do any of these factors enter into the suicide of your loved one? While this situation alone does not account for the death, it may be a circumstance that helps you get some understanding of why your loved one died.[8]

Mental illness is associated with suicide in over 90 percent of completed suicides. Psychological autopsy studies verify this figure over and over again. The relationship between depression and

---

8   See chapter 5 for a more in-depth treatment of the *Why* question.

suicide is particularly strong in that a clinically depressed person is over 50 percent more likely to attempt suicide than someone without this depression. These statistics are not surprising; they verify common sense and the usual belief that someone who takes her own life is "not in her right mind." This was clearly the case with Karla. How does this statistic fit with your experience?

This next statistic is difficult for those of us who are grieving the suicide of a loved one. The research finding maintains that the large majority of people who died by suicide left cues and warnings about their intention to kill themselves. Many of us saw some of the warnings, and yet we could not prevent the death. We will address this terrible feeling of guilt in chapter 2, but for now it is enough to state that researchers have identified some of these cues. With Karla, we saw the signs many times and took whatever action we could, but at the end we did not think she was as vulnerable as she was. Often we look back and see things that we didn't recognize at the time. It is not fair to judge ourselves by what we know now and transfer that knowledge back in time and hold ourselves accountable for what we see today but did not see before the suicide.

Those of us who lost a loved one to suicide are called suicide survivors. That is not my term, and I discuss this designation a little later in this chapter. Although the number of survivors is difficult to calculate, conservative estimates indicate that there are at least six survivors for every completed suicide. Based on data from 1983 to 2010, we can estimate that the number of survivors in the United States is approximately 4.78 million (one of every sixty-five Americans in 2010.) An estimated 230,184 survivors of suicide were added in 2010. We are clearly not alone in our grief, although it often feels like we are alone. Many people who suffer from this grief do not speak about it because of the stigma attached to suicide, and because friends, coworkers, and sometimes even family members do not know how to process this grief, or even how to talk about it. This book is an effort to help us through this grief.

The statistics, research findings, and conclusions in this section are based on the information found on the website of the American Association of Suicidology.[9] Please check this site and the previous site identified in this section if you want more information about who the people are who die by suicide.

The Language of Suicide

How do we deal with these statistics and research findings? How do we even talk about suicide and suicide survivors in a way that is honest and helpful? We begin by clarifying the language we use when we talk about suicide.

Language is our primary means of communication. Language flows from human experience, and ideally, our language accurately reflects our experience and thoughts. We go through something and then we search our vocabulary to find suitable words to describe that event.

One problem with this natural process is that we inherit language regarding our experience. Fortunately, we don't start from scratch when we try to describe what happens to us. We borrow the language from people who have had the experience before us. We use their language to describe our experience. This process is inevitable and valuable. Otherwise, we would all have to create our own language to express what happens, which would end up in communication chaos. Our common language allows us to communicate more clearly.

---

9   http://www.suicidology.org/c/document_library/get_
     file?folderId=248&name=DLFE-618.pdf.

A difficulty emerges, however, when we experience something that our inherited language doesn't accurately or completely express. We then try to force our experience into accepted language. Sometimes the language does not adequately reflect the experience, which is one reason why our language adds new words each year and deletes other words that no longer apply. Language lives and grows because human experience transcends the words we use to describe that experience.

The suicide of a loved one is a case in point. There are at least three areas where it might be helpful to explore some new ways to speak about suicide and suicide grief: *suicide survivors, suicide veterans,* and *died by suicide.* This verbal exploration may help us describe our experience of the suicide of a loved one more accurately and thereby help us grieve more effectively.

Suicide Survivors

I presume that many of the people who read *The Unique Grief of Suicide* are suicide survivors like me. As the final item in the research findings above indicates, there are millions of us. While the large number of suicide survivors is somewhat consoling because we are not alone in our loss, it does little to take away the feelings of grief that we endure each day.

Even though I have no substitute phrase, I don't particularly like the term *suicide survivors* to designate those of us who lost a loved one to suicide. Hearing the term for the first time, most people think that the survivor is someone who attempted suicide but did not succeed. That interpretation is fair enough; it is how we generally use the word *survivor*. To *survive* means to stay alive, endure, recover after an accident, live through a war or a hurricane, or, on a lighter note, a final exam or a TV series. We do not normally or immediately think of a survivor as someone who lives after someone else dies.

It is annoying, distracting, and sometimes painful to explain the meaning of the phrase *suicide survivor* to a friend who wants to comfort you after the suicide of a loved one. It feels like going into teacher mode when all you can do is struggle with your conflicting emotions. I use the term as little as possible because I know that whenever I use it, I have to explain it. The phrase itself becomes an obstacle.

It isn't only that *suicide survivor* is hard to explain. The purpose of the phrase is to describe the feelings of a person who loses a loved one to suicide. The words insist that we are surviving, barely getting through the ordeal, loss, and pain of trying to cope with the death. The term sometimes seems to be accurate enough to reflect those initial reactions to the loss. For months after Karla's death, surviving emotionally was barely possible, even though at work I was developing and implementing one of the largest projects I ever directed in my life. I'm still not sure how I "survived" and even performed well professionally.

But I simply am not comfortable thinking of myself and being referred to as a survivor. Is it denial? Perhaps, but I don't think so. My best guess is that I always felt, as bad as the immediate aftermath of Karla's death was, that I was doing more than surviving. Surviving what? I was never suicidal myself. Surviving the grief, the loss? I knew I would survive in the sense that life was going to continue in some way and I was going to be a part of it. I was certainly not coping well, or managing, or thriving, but I was not as bad as merely surviving either.

It was more like making sure I would get through each day meeting my basic responsibilities with as much efficiency as I could muster. I would periodically break down and cry, lose my focus, but then I would recover and move on to the next hour, the next task, the next conversation, the next day, until the series of nexts added up to days, weeks, and months. During that time, I felt I was doing more than surviving, and any objective observer would probably agree.

Some people suggest that we simply use the phrase *suicide griever*, and that verbiage may work for you, too. It is accurate, but it hasn't caught on among the people I know and in most of the literature I've seen. The suicide survivor label is more entrenched in our society at this point.

But since I have no other alternative phrase, and since *suicide survivor* is the accepted term in the world of suicide grief, I do not and will not make an issue about how we are labeled. It is a phrase that apparently fits many of us, and I certainly don't want to tamper with it or suggest that it isn't accurate or comforting to others. But it doesn't really fit for me, and I struggle to find better words that do fit. In the meantime I will continue to say *suicide survivor* or *suicide griever*.

Suicide Veterans

The introduction of the term *suicide veteran* is an attempt to describe my grief after the initial shock and after working through the original grief somewhat successfully. I experience grief differently now than I did during those first two years. My grief today remains, but it is different, and *suicide veteran* seems a more accurate expression of my current experience.

The dictionary says that a *veteran* is "a person of long experience in some service or position, especially in military service," which is the common understanding of the term. We use the word *veteran* in many ways. Veteran ballplayers are people who still play the game but, presumably, have more experience, wisdom, and know-how, even if their skills are not as great as those of a rookie. There are veteran teachers, plumbers, doctors, and truck drivers. It's a term of respect, acknowledging that they have overcome some hurdles and are accomplished in their field. Many military veterans testify to the deep-seated impact of their military experience, and they join organizations like the Veterans of Foreign Wars in order to remember their military service and to continue aspects of that service into the present. The term *veteran* is an honored title, and implies that a person made it through a difficult experience that has a continuing impact on his life.

Suicide veterans, then, are people who survived the initial shock and pain of the suicide of a loved one and who now feel the pain differently. Never forgetting their loved one, they emerged from the original grief with some level of acceptance and integration, and now live a relatively peaceful life, without guilt, shame, or the devastating, overwhelming sense of loss that originally dominated their lives. They assimilated the suicide into their lives. They are forever changed because of the suicide, and the hole in their hearts cannot be filled. It is still pain, but a transformed pain—an absorbed pain.

The evolution from suicide survivor to suicide veteran varies with each person because all loss is unique. It generally takes years and a lot of hard grief work. There will likely be relapses to the survivor experience. But the pain can change from devastating to manageable. The goal of suicide survivor grief work is to become a suicide veteran, someone who has assimilated the death into his life. The transition from suicide survivor to veteran may be language that reflects this changing experience.

Died by Suicide

The most common way we refer to suicide is to say or write that "_____ committed suicide." *Commit* is a harsh verb; we commit a crime or commit a sin. That same accusatory connotation carries over when we apply it to suicide. As a result, our most common phrase about suicide prejudges a person who carries out the act as guilty. We automatically disregard the overwhelming psychological pain a person who dies by suicide experiences, and we at least imply that the person deserves some form of punishment. The message is that the person committed a crime or a sin, and even though he may not have been thinking right at the time of death, he retains some significant guilt.

It is time to erase the phrase *committed suicide* from our thinking and vocabulary. A more exact and sensitive way to say it is that _____ "died by suicide," or "died from mental illness," or "completed suicide." This is not just a matter of being politically correct in our speech. It is a matter of speaking accurately about the experience of suicide and erasing some of the stigma attached to suicide.

But *committed suicide* is so deeply ingrained in our society that it is hard to eliminate; it even shows up inadvertently in the language of suicide survivors and veterans. Some hints on how to erase the phrase from our language might be helpful:

1. It is hard to change this language and thought habit alone. Make a pact with your family and friends to gently remind each other when anyone uses the term. Awareness that we are using the phrase is the first step toward eliminating it.

2. Make a decision that you will always say "died by suicide" or an equivalent. Then take a few minutes to reinforce that decision in your head.

3. When you are alone and perhaps looking into a mirror, practice saying "died by suicide." In the early stages of grief, it is difficult for many people to even say the word *suicide*. When you are ready, listen to yourself saying "died by suicide" until you are comfortable with the phrasing.

4. Check e-mails and letters before you send them to make sure your language is appropriate.

5. If you are able, when you see the phrase *committed suicide* in print or hear it on the radio or TV, write or call the media outlet to inform them that the phrasing is inappropriate.

Language matters. Perhaps *suicide veterans* and *died by suicide* are two phrases that more accurately reflect the reality of suicide and suicide grief. If all of us use the better phrasing *died by suicide* or *completed suicide* consistently, we can gradually erase the damning *committed suicide* and create a more enlightened and less stigma-producing public.

Suicide and Mental Illness

The research referenced earlier indicates that "90% of people who die by suicide have a diagnosable and treatable psychiatric disorder at the time of their death."[10] This finding is not surprising, and I like to believe that the general public recognizes the role that mental illness plays in suicide. Since the desire to live is so strong, people seem to accept that something must be seriously wrong with those who contradict that innate desire and take their own lives. The statistics verify that core belief; there is something seriously wrong with them. As a society we talk about committing suicide but, at the same time, we know that mental illness interferes with sound judgment. It seems we are ambivalent about assigning guilt to those who die by suicide.

What is not ambivalent is that most survivors not only live with the suicide of a loved one, but also, before the suicide, lived with someone with mental health problems. The frustration and strain of loving a person with mental illness is often overwhelming, and

---

10   American Foundation for Suicide Prevention, http://www.afsp.org/index. cfm?page_id=04ea1254-bd31-1fa3-c549d77e6ca6aa37.

most suicide survivors experienced that frustration for many years prior to the suicide. In fact, over the years, a few people in our suicide survivor support group admitted that they felt some relief when their loved one died. The struggle of trying to cope with the depression, or mania, or impulsive, erratic, and sometimes aggressive behavior wore them out and left them exhausted, angry, and nearly hopeless. They claimed that the suicide brought some "peace" to their loved one, but also to them. They expressed guilt that they felt this way, but in their honesty, they insisted that this sense of relief was genuine.

This reaction is surely not shared by all suicide survivors. I never felt it. But it is the truth for some survivors. What it demonstrates is the extent to which the mental illness prior to the suicide impacts the grief of the survivors. It isn't just the suicide that survivors deal with; it is the life before the suicide also. That combination of feelings complicates the grieving process.

Some people die by suicide without any identifiable indications of mental illness. When there is no history of a diagnosable mental disorder, the survivors have to deal with the death with no clear condition that might help explain the suicide. A situation like this introduces a whole new set of complications, particularly when the "Why did they do it?" question arises.[11]

The point here is that most survivors must incorporate their experience of the mental illness along with the sudden and violent death of their loved one into their lives. This inclusion is just another reason why suicide grief is unique.

---

11   See chapter 5.

Alcoholism, Substance Abuse, and Suicide

In drawing a picture of those who die by suicide and those they leave behind, we must acknowledge the role that alcohol and substance abuse plays in suicide. As the research findings indicated, "The risk of suicide in alcoholics is 50 to 70 percent higher than the general population."[12] Alcoholism is a terrible disease that can ultimately lead to a depression that robs people of the will to live. Reducing alcoholism reduces the number of suicides.

Alcoholism and substance abuse are often coupled with mental illness because people self-medicate in order to try to cope with the mental disorder. The drugs and alcohol help a person with depression, schizophrenia, bipolar, or other brain disorders escape from the effects of the disease, only to lead them to an added debilitating illness. The result is co-occurring disorders—the mental illness and the addiction. This combination is a high-risk prescription for suicide.

This combination of mental illness and substance abuse statistically affects millions of people. Since these issues increase the risk of suicide, they are a significant part of the profile of those who die by suicide. As a result, they are also a significant part of the issues facing survivors.

Those Who Died

Suicide occurs in every economic segment, all age groups, both genders, all religious groups, every race, and is a part of any other demographic grouping in our society. It is not confined to lower social standing, poverty, education levels, or religious affiliation. Suicide is a non-discriminatory event. And the grief following

---

12   http://www.suicidology.org/c/document_library/get_
file?folderId=262&name=DLFE-625.pdf.

a suicide is common to all survivors, usually erasing all social distinctions.

On the other hand, the statistics offer a glimpse at who is more susceptible to suicide. It isn't that the numbers give us a probable profile of who will complete suicide, but they do provide us with some clues as to which sets of circumstances might lead to suicide. We can be more vigilant in watching, and therefore possibly preventing, some suicides with those higher-risk people. Those of us who are survivors are also ardent supporters of suicide prevention. We don't wish this grief on anyone else.

One of the obvious realities about our loved ones who died by suicide is that they are dead. Their death makes us survivors. They may or may not fit the profile of someone who was likely to complete suicide. In any case, the harsh truth is that they have died.

This whole book is a response to that core reality. Here I want to mention this death in its broadest terms so that we may move away from the temptation to describe and remember our loved ones through the narrow window of how they died. That temptation is very strong, almost overwhelming, in the beginning of our grief.

Some of the above statistics may apply to your loved one. What the statistics demonstrate is that our loved ones are much more than their deaths. To remember their lives, we must minimize their deaths. I am not speaking of denial; I am speaking of perspective. They are not defined by their death; their lives, even in the worst times, were more than their illness. It is that perspective, more than anything else, that transforms us from survivors to suicide veterans.

To make that transition it is helpful to consciously recall scenes, conversations, and events that activate happy memories. For me, it's remembering the many talks I had with Karla about philosophy, theology, history, literature, and writing. Then there is always the memory of the two of us fishing together during our annual family vacations. There remain fond memories of car trips throughout eastern Oklahoma that she and I took when she was a preteen and I was making presentations or holding meetings in cities three or four hours away from Tulsa.

These memories are a part of me, and are not connected with her death. Immediately after her death, these kinds of memories were painful in that they reminded me of the happy times, and I wanted those times back. But slowly the pleasant memories found a place of their own, divorced from her suicide. It isn't that I discovered some magic technique that forced the separation of the good times from the bad times. All I did was recall the good times and view them as good times. Eventually these thoughts gained legitimacy and credibility, and were able to stand on their own, without reference to the memories of the difficult times with her bipolar disorder and her suicide. Gradually, along with the reality of her death, came the reality of her life. The suicide statistical profile which fits her does not encompass all of her. I hope that all people who grieve a suicide experience a similar transition.

Other People

Besides the person who died and those of us left behind, there are other people, a broad category that includes all of society, but more specifically those people who know us. For most of us, the extended family (cousins, aunts, uncles, grandparents, siblings, etc.) and coworkers, neighbors, and friends are these other people. When they hear of the suicide, they want to console us, but most of them don't know how to do it. The stigma of suicide is still very strong, and misunderstanding regarding the why and how of the death is evident.

Sometimes these people will say things that hurt us. It is not intentional, but I have heard some of it myself: "Karla cannot go to heaven." "Suicide is a very selfish act." "Why didn't you stop it?" While most comments are not that bold, survivors know what people mean when they make similar remarks. And it hurts. I usually just let the comments go without any response because I don't want an argument, especially about my daughter's suicide. But it hurts. Occasionally, years later, I will gently confront people who say these things, just to set the record straight and try to reduce the stigma.

Most often these other people just don't understand suicide and the grief that follows. The implication in many of these comments is that we didn't love her well enough. We failed her. We didn't listen to her, had too many expectations of her, let her down, didn't support her well enough, did not approve of her. The meaning is that we are guilty. If we are parents, we are bad parents. They want to console us, but the consolation takes the form of pity for us because we failed her and now we have to live with those consequences for the rest of our lives. It's a harsh condemnation, and fortunately, it doesn't happen too often. But it only needs to happen a few times to have a demoralizing impact. My guess is that most survivors have experienced something like this.

Most people do not make or even think these condemnatory remarks. They simply don't know what to say or do. They cannot imagine what it would be like if they were in our shoes. Death leaves mourners. But with other deaths, there is a clear, identifiable cause of death. That clarity evaporates with suicide. Most people do not automatically think that mental illness causes death, even though they immediately accept that cancer causes death. It is even more difficult to console a survivor when there was no diagnosed mental illness prior to the suicide. As a result, people have difficulty consoling suicide survivors.

What you tell other people about the suicide is, of course, your decision. We were very open about Karla's suicide mainly because she was open about her mental illness. We went so far as writing her obituary in such a way that readers knew how she died. There are advantages to being honest about the suicide:

- You don't have to spend emotional energy pretending it wasn't suicide.

- You may wind up saying different things to different people and then not remembering what you said to whom. Trying to keep your message straight over the years adds more pressure and tension.

- If children are involved, it seems best to tell them what happened in age-appropriate language, but you don't want the child to learn about the suicide from some other source in the future.

- If you are honest about the death, then your friends and family can support you better. Besides, it is a relief to share your genuine grief with others.

All things considered, it seems better to tell people the truth about what happened.

Feelings of shame and guilt are the likely reason why people want to keep the suicide a secret. But the cover-up, the secret, and the pretending will likely cause more problems than the supposed shame and guilt. Trust most other people to respond with compassion when you tell them the truth, because that is probably what will happen, and you will be better supported. Don't associate with people who do not accept the truth and who judge you negatively. There will be many more who will console you in whatever way they can. Go to them.

Hope

There are no answers to some questions related to suicide. But the lack of answers does not mean that there is a lack of hope. The death is final; that's the harsh reality. But as my wife, Fran, says, "Karla took her life; I can't let her take mine." Wise words that form the basis for hope for us survivors.

All the statistics in this chapter can be discouraging. So many people dying by suicide! Will we ever be able to stop the self-slaughter? We who are suicide survivors hope that the more people speak out about suicide, the better our suicide prevention efforts will be. And the people who have the greatest credibility in suicide prevention programs are the suicide survivors and veterans.

We will never be able to get over the suicide of a loved one, but we can get through it. Typically, the initial few months and years are the hardest. It will never get worse than those years. Time does not heal automatically, but time ushers in new experiences, and time makes us do other things that are not related to the suicide. We relate to our families and friends; we go to work; we buy groceries; we pay the bills; we make decisions; we talk to people; we read books; we watch TV. The accumulation of these experiences pushes our initial focus on suicide to the side, even if only momentarily at first.

The hole in our lives due to the suicide gradually gets surrounded by so many ongoing experiences that we do not consciously focus on the suicide as much. The hole seems to shrink but never disappears. It creates a permanent scar that opens periodically but then re-seals.

Time alone does not heal; time alone simply makes us older, and we get more accustomed to the grief we continue to feel. Time plus grief work offers the best chance to assimilate the suicide into our ongoing lives. There is always a sadness that accompanies our suicide memories, but that sadness can mix

31

with other genuine happy memories of our loved one and other joyful events and experiences. The process from devastation to assimilation is difficult, and most of us need help along the way. It is not something we usually accomplish on our own. But it does happen, and suicide veterans will testify to its reality.

That process begins with honesty—honesty about the suicide and about our feelings regarding the suicide. Since everyone grieves in their own way and in their own time, there are no prescribed stages or steps that lead to assimilation, but it happens. The hope is based on trusting that process.

Questions for Personal Reflection or Group Discussion

1. What are the similarities and differences in the story of your loved one as compared with Karla's story? If you are not a suicide survivor, what drew your attention to Karla's story?

2. What two statistics struck you the most and why?

3. How does the term *suicide survivor* fit with your experience of suicide?

4. How does the term *suicide veteran* fit with your experience?

5. What is your feeling about the common phrase *committed suicide*?

6. If it applies to you, to what extent does the mental illness of your loved one impact your suicide grief?

7. To what extent was alcohol or substance abuse a part of your loved one's suicide?

8. To what extent are you able to view your loved one in a complete context, focusing not just on the suicide?

9. How have other people responded to the suicide of your loved one?

10. To what extent have you been open about the suicide of your loved one?

11. To what extent are you hopeful that you will become a suicide veteran?

CHAPTER 2

Suicide and Suicide Grief

THE *WHAT* QUESTION

Suicide is not as clear-cut as it may seem. It is the act of taking one's own life, and in most cases, it is obvious that the death is self-inflicted and intended. That is clearly the fact with Karla's suicide.

But other situations are more complicated, which is why law enforcement personnel, medical examiners, and coroners initially assume that apparent suicides are actually homicides and begin the investigation of the death from that perspective. While this approach is understandable from a legal viewpoint, it can cause additional stress for the family and friends of the deceased as they struggle with the immediate impact of the death. Though we had no doubt that Karla died by suicide, we waited three days before the medical examiner in Tulsa officially declared that she killed herself by "a perforating gunshot wound to the chest." It took another two days to ship her body from Tulsa to Belleville, Illinois. Her wake was on the Friday after her Monday death, with the funeral on Saturday. The timing worked out for us, but the delay in determining the cause of death adds another complex problem on top of the usual difficulties that accompany a sudden death and planning for a funeral.

For the record, *Webster's New Twentieth Century Dictionary Unabridged Second Edition* describes suicide as "the act of killing oneself intentionally." The intention of the person is the pivotal point. When people knowingly place themselves in a position where they will die but in doing so, they save the lives of others, we call that act courageous, not suicide. Throwing yourself on a grenade to save others, or taking a bullet in order to protect a family member or a president, or jumping out of an overloaded boat so it doesn't sink, are all examples of knowing you are going to die, but the act is not suicide.

Some movie critics and viewers claim that though the Will Smith character in the movie *Seven Pounds* died by suicide, it was a redeemed suicide because he donated his body parts to help other people. Did his intention justify his suicide? On a similar note, no Christian would say that because Jesus knew he was going to be killed when he went to Jerusalem to confront the authorities that he died by suicide.

In recent decades, suicide in the news is often linked with suicide bombers. These deaths are intended as a political statement, terrorist tactic, and a weapon to kill others. They are not suicides in the same category as, for example, Karla's death, and I resent even sharing the word suicide with them.

Since intention is the key concept in the definition of suicide, when that intention is clouded, the suicide is also clouded. As we shall see in a later chapter ("Chapter 5: Grieving—The *Why* Question"), research says that people usually take their own lives in order to end the psychological pain or emotional stress they are experiencing. They don't really want to die; they want to end the pain and taking their own lives is the only way they know, at that time, how to stop the pain. Their intention then is not straightforward suicide. Do they still fit the definition of suicide when the intentionality is so mixed?

Suicide, therefore, is not as precise as we might assume. On the other hand, for most of us who are suicide grievers, we know what we mean by the suicide of our loved one, and distinctions about the official definition are not relevant or helpful. I only mention them here for those survivors or veterans who find themselves in an unclear situation regarding the suicide.

Grief Emotions of Suicide Survivors

When a loved one dies by suicide, the grief by each person affected is unique. And the multiple emotions that emerge are often intense, intermingled, and devastating. Sorting out those feelings, coping with them one at time, or even harder, all of them together, is a daunting challenge for anyone, even for a balanced, mature person. The suicidal death of a loved one creates an abnormal emotional reaction that no one can anticipate or prepare for. Those feelings emerge, filtered through our personalities, and remain roaming around inside us for an unpredictable period of time and intensity.

Many people find it helpful to name the emotions associated with the loss. One path to healthy recovery from grief is to *name* and then *claim* these feelings as our own. This journey of naming and claiming can be long and difficult. If we are people who are not accustomed to identifying our feelings, the suicide experience and its accompanying emotions can wreak havoc on our lives for a long time. If we usually bury our feelings and then also bury our shock, anger, depression, loss, guilt, or loneliness due to the suicide, we run the risk of these negative reactions becoming a permanent part of our personality. Most counselors, psychiatrists, ministers, social workers, and people of wisdom advise us to try to name and claim these emotions as a critical step in our grief journey.

Once we name and claim these feelings, it is crucial that someone else accepts, honors, and validates these emotions. Often, a counselor does this validation best.

The following sections attempt to categorize and describe feelings that often accompany suicide. These are not stages of grief. One does not automatically lead to another, nor do they progress chronologically. The order and intensity of the feelings can vary, with new emotions rising to the forefront while others recede. One feeling may reemerge after it was reconciled previously, and some of these emotions do not apply to everyone. Other feelings not described here may also be critical, and individual circumstances and relationships may introduce other emotions that need attention.

Whatever the feelings are and whatever the circumstances, it is valuable to identify these emotions accurately and to claim them as our own honestly. Without this effort to name and claim, the worst of the suicide grief process will take longer and result in more negative effects than necessary. With this focus, grief will lose some of its power, and we will be able to assimilate the suicide into our life more thoroughly and quickly.

Shock and Denial
I can't believe it, and I feel numb.

That's how many of us describe our initial reaction to the news of the suicide of our loved one. The following quote is the definition of *acute stress reaction* which is a more precise term for what we refer to as shock.

A transient disorder that develops in an individual without any other apparent mental disorder in response to exceptional physical and mental stress and that usually subsides within hours or days. Individual vulnerability and coping capacity play a role in the occurrence and severity of acute stress reactions. The symptoms show a typically mixed and changing picture and include an initial state of 'daze' with some constriction of the field of consciousness and narrowing of attention, inability to comprehend stimuli, and disorientation. This state may be followed either by further withdrawal from the surrounding situation (to the extent of dissociative stupor-F44.2), or by agitation and over-activity (flight reaction or fugue). Autonomic signs of panic anxiety (tachycardia, sweating, flushing) are commonly present. The symptoms usually appear within minutes of the impact of the stressful stimulus or event, and disappear within two to three days (often with hours). Partial or complete amnesia (F44.0) for the episode may be present. If the symptoms persist, a change in diagnosis should be considered.[13]

The suicide of a loved one clearly fits the description of shock (acute stress reaction) as outlined in the previous paragraph. But I use the word *shock* more loosely than the more specific definition. At times, I am still stunned by Karla's death; I believe it, but I am still sometimes shocked by her absence. It is helpful to know the general, medical description of shock in order to know that it no longer applies to me. But the broader use of the word still conveys one aspect of my ongoing reaction to her death. Other feelings and words more accurately reflect my current emotions, and I speak of them much more often than I use the word *shock*. But occasionally, it feels appropriate to say that I am still shocked by her suicide.

---

13   *International Classification of Diseases-10 (ICD-10)*, F-43. World Health Organization, United Nations, 2012. The ICD-10 is the standard diagnostic tool for epidemiology, health management and clinical purposes.

Denial is another word that doesn't apply to me. I cannot deny that Karla died by suicide. She did. In other cases the evidence may not be so definite. If you suspect homicide or accidental death, then denial might be appropriate. But when all the evidence points to suicide, it is better in the long run not to deny it.

When suicide survivors speak, we sometimes use the word denial to refer to those feelings that resist acceptance of the reality of the death. Early on in suicide grief, there are occasions when the loss is so painful that we try to deny the loss. We shove those feelings aside or try to stuff them deep within us so we don't have to face them. We sometimes refer to that experience as denial. It is not denying the death; it's refusing to accept the pain. While denial is not the clearest way to express this unfamiliar and intense pain, it is a word that can be useful when we can't find a better way to name and claim our emotions.

Frustration

I can't understand why my loved one died by suicide. I see other alternatives, and I am haunted by the unanswered questions surrounding the reason for the death.

The frustration generated by a suicide is predictable and understandable. Frustration implies that a personal goal cannot be achieved. Our goal for our loved ones is that they live, but suddenly they are dead by their own hand. Our goal is not elaborate, remarkable, or extraordinary. It is as basic as a goal can be. We simply wanted our loved ones to be alive. That basic fact is no longer the case, not by an accident, or a physical disease, but by a stigmatized brain disorder, a convoluted, unintelligible, baffling mental illness that convinced them that death was the only way to solve the problem of life. In some cases the suicide seems like an impulsive, blinding, literally thoughtless act of self-destruction, a permanent solution to a temporary problem. It is normal to feel frustration when our simple goal that they remain alive is shattered.

Sometimes we think of frustration as a minor feeling. Traffic doesn't move as fast as we want. Our team loses a big game. A child's report card doesn't meet expectations. Our health slows us down. A relationship ends. We experience frustration often and in varying degrees. But the frustration associated with suicide is deep-seated, pervasive, and certainly not minor. If we let it fester, it can ruin our lives. It deserves to be named and claimed in order to lessen its impact on us.

Anger

I feel angry at the deceased, at myself, at other people, at God, at the world.

Anger is common among suicide grievers. But it is often a diffused anger since we are not sure who deserves our anger. Anger at our deceased loved one is often mixed with our sadness and loss. We are sometimes angry at ourselves, feeling that we could have done something to prevent the suicide. Some of our anger overflows onto others, either because of our own frustration or because we feel other people could have prevented the death. Some people are angry at their concept of God because they feel their God let them down by allowing their loved one to take his own life. The anger can be so diffused that we end up angry at everyone and everything.

We usually think of anger as a loud, emotional response to some provocation, with retaliation in mind. It sometimes includes an adrenaline rush, increased heart rate, and the impulse to strike back at someone or something, either physically or verbally. It is expressed in words, body language, threatening posture, or aggressive acts. It often implies losing control over normal thinking, which can lead to spontaneous and regrettable behavior.

This type of anger is understandable for suicide survivors. The suicide is such a violent and permanent destruction of a relationship that anger is an appropriate response. The force of this anger may be so foreign to a specific person that its overwhelming impact may be a totally new sensation. If people are not accustomed to the intensity of this feeling they may not know how to control or manage the anger.

Suicide anger can also take a different course. The anger may not be instantaneously intense but still very real. We talk about a slow, seething anger; a steady feeling of wanting to strike back; and a severe desire to erupt emotionally. But we don't give in to that desire. We hold back the force of our anger, but we don't lose the anger. Even if we admit that we are angry, we don't know what to do with it or how to get rid of it. We sometimes transfer the suicide anger to some other lesser provocation and try to release the emotional pressure indirectly. That tactic usually doesn't work, and soon we are seething again. The suicide is the occasion for the anger, but we can't change the suicide, so we think we can't change the anger. For many of us, this type of anger is more common than the immediate, explosive type.

Like all of the suicide emotions, the first step to defusing our anger is to name it and claim it. Admit and accept the anger, not judgmentally but honestly. Identify who or what we are angry at as precisely as possible. Take time to become aware of our anger and focus on the specifics. Self-awareness is essential to suicide grief work. And it is nowhere more needed than in this area of diffused anger.

We own our anger, like we own all our feelings. The suicide doesn't cause our anger; it is the occasion which triggers our own angry reaction. *I* am angry. I can also choose to let my anger go, to let it dissipate and disintegrate. That choice is not easy but it starts with awareness of how these feelings originate. They come from me; I am the subject who creates these emotions. It is often a difficult process, but I can also change my feelings, even my anger.

Rejection

I feel abandoned by the suicide. I am deeply hurt that my loved one wanted to die more than wanting to be with me.

The feeling of rejection is one of the most difficult emotions to cope with in the wake of a suicide. It's hard to get past the fact that a loved one thought it was better to die than to remain connected to us. We have all felt rejection at some point in life: last chosen for a team, shunned by the "in crowd," denied a relationship, lost a good job, turned down on a proposal. Rejection is a part of life, and a mature person learns to live with it and grows emotionally from the experience.

But suicide is a rejection that cuts so deep and lasts so long that it continually haunts us. It helps to recognize and believe that our loved one didn't really intend to reject us. Karla told us two weeks before she died that she was a burden on us and that we and the universe would be better off without her. We, of course, tried to show her that she was wrong, that we loved her and wanted her. In the end, she followed her twisted way of thinking, but I believe it wasn't because she deliberately rejected us. She saw no other way out.

That line of thinking helps shrink the feeling of rejection, but it doesn't eliminate it. Her solution rejects us. That hurt lives. That pain survives, even though she didn't.

Once again, naming the rejection is a step toward accepting it. Part of the suicide grief journey is becoming a little more comfortable with this feeling of rejection, not letting it dominate our lives. To name it and claim it takes some of the sting out of it.

Isolation

I want to tell the rest of the world to leave me alone. I seem so unorganized and disoriented, and I don't care. Just being with other people is overwhelming.

Sometimes after a suicide, just being with other people, even other people we love, is too demanding. We need space to try to get some perimeters on our sorrow, but it is hard to contain and takes all of our emotional energy just to exist with the loss and the questions. We want to be alone, not to solve the problem, but because we have never experienced anything like this, we don't know how to react or what to do. We think, "Just stay away and leave me alone."

Other responsibilities in life seem irrelevant. Work and family needs barely exist, and even if we go through the motions, our heart, mind, energy, and focus are consumed by our loss. We may have experienced significant grief before with the death of other loved ones, but suicide cuts deeper, has more jagged edges, and tears us apart in emotional, intellectual, social, spiritual, and physical areas we didn't know we had. We can't keep anything else together; and we may do some basic things, but only because our body memory knows how to do them without thinking. It's no wonder we want to spend much of our time in isolation.

Even if we are very responsible people, it may be that we don't really care about anything else. Suicide puts a perspective on life that shrinks the importance of everything except the death. What else can matter? Work can get along without me. Family relationships can be ignored. The rest of the world can go away. Who cares?

Depression

I realize all that has been or will be lost. I experience
unusual sadness and helplessness. I have little
or no motivation. I can't eat or sleep.

Some level of depression is likely for suicide survivors. How do I know if my depression is normal following a suicide or if I am clinically depressed?

If the depression has symptoms like constant sadness, irritability, hopelessness, trouble sleeping, low energy or fatigue, feeling worthless or guilty for no reason, significant weight change, difficulty concentrating, and loss of interest in favorite activities, you may be clinically depressed. These are the symptoms identified in the *Diagnostic and Statistical Manual of Mental Disorders—IV*[14] for major depressive disorder. When five of these symptoms are present for most of the day, nearly every day for at least two weeks, a mental health professional would likely diagnose depression and start an appropriate treatment plan. At least one of the symptoms must be either persistent sad or "empty" feelings or loss of interest in activities.

If you meet these criteria, it is wise to see a mental health professional. Even if you don't qualify for a clinical depression diagnosis, it still might be wise to talk to a counselor about your grief. The suicidal death of a loved one is a severe blow to your life, and seeking help in coping with the impact of this loss is not a disgrace or negative comment about you. A counselor may be necessary to regain your balance.

The sadness, helplessness, low motivation, and inability to eat or sleep are common reactions to a suicide, and they will likely

---

14   *Diagnostic and Statistical Manual of Mental Disorders–IV* (American Psychiatric Association, 2000). This work is commonly abbreviated DSM-IV-TR.

remain for varying lengths of time for different people. The intensity of the depression will likely lessen in time and with the support of grief work. But it is possible that some level of periodic sadness will be a permanent part of life. It need not be debilitating, but it may emerge at various times. Even years later, it may come to the surface, sometimes disguised as some other form of sadness. Whenever it does surface, it remains important to name it accurately in order to deal with it properly.

Guilt and Shame

If only I had, or had not. I feel like a failure as a parent, a spouse, a friend. I am embarrassed by the suicide. I experience regrets.

It's rare that some form of guilt, shame or regret doesn't accompany a suicide. Why didn't I fly to Tulsa to be with Karla the weekend before she died? As I mentioned in chapter 1, she was released against our wishes from a behavioral health care center on a Friday with an aggressive aftercare plan beginning on Monday afternoon. She was in treatment for ten days for severe depression. If I had been with her over that weekend, would she still have shot herself? I will never know, but I do regret not going to Tulsa that weekend.

None of us really know if we could have prevented the suicide of our loved one. Some of us tried hard for years to stop the suicide, ultimately to no avail. Some of us had no idea that the suicide would happen, but we still replay that last day, the last hour, thinking we could have done something to prevent the tragedy. What if I had done this or that? What if I picked up on some warning signs more clearly? What if I had made a phone call at the right time? Or, what if I had loved her better?

These are all questions without answers. But they can still haunt us. We must ask those questions because they are within us, roaming around in our emotional life, seeking answers, finding blame, and destroying our peace. Keep asking the questions out loud to someone you trust. In time you will likely not have to ask them anymore because you know you did the best you could at the time, and that you never intended to ignore your loved one so that he could kill himself. Our feelings of guilt, though sometimes very strong, have no basis in reality. We must forgive ourselves because we did nothing wrong. We did not cause our loved one's death. We may or may not have been able to prevent this suicide, or a later suicide, but the fact is we didn't prevent this one, not because we didn't want to but because we simply couldn't. It isn't our fault.

Loneliness

I feel forgotten and alone. No one understands
what I'm going through.

Often loneliness accompanies the feelings of rejection and isolation. When I think about the things I would have done with Karla, the conversations, the trips, sharing her life and my life as we both grew older, her education, probable marriage and children, I am lonely and miss her. I also miss other people who have died—my parents, brother and sister in particular—but Karla's suicide is different. She could have lived but didn't. That loneliness is unique.

No one else really understands my feelings of loneliness for her. I cannot explain it, and at its deepest level, I cannot share it. I ache, but the ache will forever be my own ache. I recognize it when it appears since I am now familiar with it, and the only way it can subside is to be present to the ache and let it slowly slip away, because it cannot sustain the intensity for too long. It simply runs out of energy after a while. And then it drifts into the deep waters of my emotions, only to resurface at some likely or unlikely time, as if it were coming up for air once again. I expect it even though I don't welcome it. But by now, I am almost comfortable with the loneliness because it is no longer a stranger—certainly not a friend, but not a diabolical enemy any more either. It is a part of my life now, a part I don't want, but a piece of me that is real, and therefore somehow valid and truthful.

I am alone in my loneliness, but I am strangely connected to Karla in those moments. It aches, but she is there in her absence. I'm not sure how this painful loneliness gradually evolved into a more acceptable form of loneliness, but that is what happened. I think it is the best I can hope for.

Searching

I start to read, talk, and seek advice, encouragement and help from others. I am looking for answers.

Most survivors start searching for answers almost immediately after the death. Many of us want to know the details surrounding the death, the circumstances, the hows, the whats, and the whys of the death. But the initial impulse to find answers is more a reflex than a serious search. We think that if we find quick answers that satisfy us sufficiently, we can speed up the painful process of grief. For most of us, the immediate desire for answers doesn't give us real relief or—that dreaded and impossible word—*closure.*

The kind of search that accompanies the feeling here is steady, serious, and purposeful. We read reputable books or articles on suicide and suicide grief. We ask for and receive help from counselors, mental health professionals, suicide grief support groups, and people we consider wise and trustworthy. Our search for answers is not a frantic attempt to eliminate the pain in our lives, but a sincere effort to understand what has happened to our loved one and what is happening to us. We know it will take time, and we are willing to be patient enough to let the information help shape our thinking and our perspective of the suicide.

This search is not necessarily a scholarly research project. It is a search that fits our personality and interests, and is only as extensive as it needs to be for us. The search goes on as long as it needs to go for our purposes; there is no preconceived ending or conclusion. For some of us, it may last years. For others, it may be shorter. But it is a search that is done calmly, with some emotion, but without stressful anxiety. Usually this kind of search is only possible months or even years after the suicide.

The benefit of this kind of search is a deeper, more rooted, and more helpful response to the death. It is extremely valuable as we move on in our lives because it provides a solid base from which we can proceed with other realities and relationships.

Assimilation

The negative feelings become less intense. I slowly begin to participate in life and enjoy some things again. I find some consolation from the special memories of my loved one.

Karla's suicide and my reaction to her death will always be a part of my life. Assimilation does not mean that this harsh reality is forgotten or dismissed. We always acknowledge that reality, and we always remember our loved one with fondness. But the death does not dominate our lives any more. We are changed forever because of this experience, but that change does not eliminate other experiences, some joyful and some sad. These other experiences receive appropriate places in our lives. Relationships grow and nourish us independently from the suicide. Activities engage us despite the death. We get older, and the circumstances of our lives evolve *regardless* of the suicide, not *because* of the suicide. In a word, we assimilate this experience into the flow of our lives.

At the beginning of the grief journey, we don't believe that this assimilation is possible. We are convinced that the suicide will dominate us forever. But if we do our grief work, assimilation is possible, as many suicide veterans insist.

Some people may refer to this feeling as *peace* or *acceptance*, and those terms may be meaningful ways to describe this emotion. But to some people, acceptance implies that they accept suicide, which they really don't do. Acceptance, to them, means that it is okay to kill yourself, and they will never agree with that proposition. It is not okay for the person who dies or for the survivors.

To assimilate the death into life does not mean you have to accept the suicide. You can assimilate it and still object to it. You can come to terms with it, and not let it interfere with your life, even as you don't accept it. You can admit it as a fact of your reality, but still not accept it. And you can still assimilate it without it undermining the rest of your life.

Other people are perfectly comfortable with the word *acceptance* and use it to describe their experience. That, too, is okay. In naming and claiming this feeling, use whichever word and meaning is most comfortable to you. The idea is for you to let this emotion become the predominate feeling associated with the suicide of your loved one, whatever you name it.

Empathy and Caring

*I know there will always be times of grieving, and I
know how hard it is to go through this. But maybe
I can help someone else through their grief.*

Outreach to others will vary from person to person. One advantage to being public and honest about the death is that other people who have experienced a suicide may feel free to talk with you about the suicide of their loved one. Since we are very open about Karla's suicide, to the point of creating the *Karla Smith Foundation* in her name, we often get questions and comments about other suicides. As the statistics in chapter 1 indicated, there are many of us.

Supporting others who are grieving a suicide benefits them, but it also helps us. For those of you who are familiar with twelve-step programs, this outreach is similar to the twelfth step. Reach out to others who have a similar experience in an effort to support and encourage them to work on their grief. Offer them your experience because this kind of sharing often brings consolation and understanding.

Perhaps the best forum for this outreach is a suicide survivor support group in your area. Involvement in it will put you in touch with other survivors quickly. You need not be a suicide bereavement counselor to help others; you simply need to be willing to share your story and your progress in a confidential but open environment. Some people refer to this reaching out as *involvement therapy* because you, too, benefit from sharing your story. In particular, if you are a suicide veteran, you can be extremely influential and supportive to people who are just beginning the suicide grief journey.

Relief

I feel some relief from the suicide because my loved one suffered for so long and now doesn't have to suffer any more. I also feel relief from my role as caregiver.

While this emotion doesn't seem widespread, occasionally someone in our support group for anyone who lost a loved one to suicide will admit that they feel some relief because of the suicide. Usually this admission is quickly followed by an expression of guilt for feeling that way. But the relief results from many years of trying to cope with some mental illness of the deceased. Chronic depression or bizarre behavior leaves many family members frustrated, confused, and angry. They also see their loved one suffer so much psychological pain, disrupted lives, institutionalization, inability to establish healthy relationships, and ongoing, unrealistic demands on caregivers, that their suicide seems a relief for their loved one and for themselves.

If this emotion is mixed in with some of the other feelings, it is best to identify it and claim it too. It may be essential to admit this relief, if it is real, in order to work through the guilt that often accompanies this feeling. Not everyone feels this way, but if you do, it is best to address it.

Suicide Grief Emotions: Conclusion

The preceding brief descriptions of twelve common emotions that accompany a suicide do not exhaust the feelings that rage or simmer within us when a loved one dies by suicide. There likely are other emotions as well. Whatever they are, it is most helpful to name them accurately, claim them as our own, and to have someone else validate them. The claiming is important because we may have a tendency to blame other people or circumstances for our negative feelings. This blaming other people or things for how we feel is a diversion and can lead us in the wrong direction for a long and destructive time. Our feelings are our own; we own them. That reality can be the major insight that leads to eventual assimilation of the suicide into our lives. That reality offers us hope and brings us balance. Without it, we will likely flounder and suffer more than is necessary.

This list of possible suicide grief emotions describes feelings that commonly occur after a suicide. Most of us who have experienced this kind of death have walked this same tortured trail. It is literally overwhelming.

However, for most of us, the intensity of these feelings will pass. The fact that you are reading this book right now means that you are taking steps to cope with your grief. How long this process takes depends on you, your coping ability, and the kind of support you receive. Eventually you will come to terms with your loss and arrive at a new sense of "normal," where the suicide does not dominate your life, and you are able to function well enough with some happiness. It certainly isn't what life was before the suicide, and you are now a changed person because of the death. For the most part, it is an acceptable new normal.

Different People: Different Grief

While naming and claiming the common emotions associated with suicide grief is a crucial part of coping with this loss, we don't all experience these emotions in the same way or to the same degree. We don't all experience these emotions in the same way or to the same degree. Since personalities differ, the grief differs. There are common elements in our grief, but there are differences as well. It is helpful to try to identify the differences as well as the common features.

Gender

A good place to begin describing the differences is with gender. While we cannot generalize that all women feel one way and all men feel another, it may be helpful to comment on some seemingly general differences in the way men and women respond to a tragedy like suicide.

Societal expectations regarding men and women have changed. Not too long ago, the ideal man in our society was emotionally remote, decisive, the head of the house, and the family provider and protector. The ideal woman was emotionally expressive, obedient to her man, the heart of her home, and the family nurturer. These profiles are stereotypes, no doubt, but true enough to influence how men and women thought of themselves and each other.

Today, of course, the roles of men and women are much more complex, to the point where the old stereotypes are no longer applicable. But in suicide grief there may remain some general gender comments that may apply in many cases.

It may be that in many family dynamics, the wife or mother assumes the greater responsibility for the emotional health of the family members. It is primarily the mother's role to address the emotional life of the children. It is mainly the mother who tries to comfort a sad child, or diffuse anger, or coach a child in relationship problems. The mother or wife becomes the central figure within the complicated balance of relationships we call family.

To the extent that this analysis is correct, the mother or wife may then assume more of the responsibility for the suicide of a family member. Since she is the center of the emotional life of the family, when a member dies by suicide, she may feel that she has failed in her role as the emotional gatekeeper. To the extent that this observation is accurate, the mother or wife has to deal with feelings of guilt after a suicide differently than the father or husband.

The father or husband, on the other hand, may consider himself the primary protector in the family. Even when both parents work outside the home, the man may still perceive his role as the one who protects the family from physical harm. When a family member dies by suicide, he may feel that he didn't protect the family well enough, and his grief will include that sense of failure.

In any case, it appears that men and women often respond to a suicide differently, and it is worth noting those differences.

Grieving a suicide becomes more complicated than necessary if one person expects another person to grieve in a way similar to him- or herself. One of the most difficult aspects of grieving is the ability to comfort other people while coping with your own unique grief. Remembering possible male and female differences may prevent unnecessary conflicts and expectations.

Grief and the Enneagram

In the final analysis, there is no such thing as grief; there are only grievers. When we describe grief, our description is already at least one step removed from the experience. Grief, and its many emotions, is an experience that is specific, personal, individual, and unique. We each experience grief in our own way and at our own pace.

When there is a death of a loved one by suicide, there are often added complications to the grief. As our look at the grief emotions indicated, suicide grievers often contend with these additional realities:

- The death appears to some degree to be a choice.
- Grievers feel abandoned and rejected.
- The death was usually sudden and often violent.
- There is real or perceived social stigma.
- There is embarrassment and isolation.
- There are many unanswered questions: Why did he or she do it?
- There are blame, regret, and a sense of responsibility.

There is value in going beyond these generalized grief emotions and searching for avenues that will help grievers identify their feelings more specifically. A more accurate, specific label for these feelings and the approach to the suicide is a helpful step toward a healthy grieving process.

The *enneagram* is one tool that can be used to describe these feelings and styles of grieving more specifically. The enneagram is a system for understanding nine basic personality types. Its proponents contend that every person is primarily one of these nine types, even though each person's unique personality is also recognized and honored.

The enneagram is complex and nuanced, but its general insights are also valuable. It is this more general understanding that forms the basis for this brief description of grief due to the suicide of a loved one. Since I am not a certified enneagram instructor and my familiarity with this system is limited, I defer to more informed enneagram experts in my analysis. But to my knowledge, no one else has ever attempted to make the connection between the enneagram and suicide grief.

According to the theory, there are nine personality types. Here's how each of these nine personality types will likely grieve the loss of a loved one who completed suicide:

1. *The Perfectionist*: the rational, idealistic type. Principled, purposeful, and self-controlled, but can be a perfectionist and self-righteous. The perfectionist (or reformer) wants to make the world perfect and has a compulsive need to live life the right way. This type will probably want to grieve the correct way—thoroughly—and will expect clear steps to mark progress. He (or she)[15] will probably be concerned about the current status of the person who died and the social stigma attached to suicide. He will grieve in an orderly, somewhat predictable manner. At their lowest, perfectionists will become

---

15   Readers should understand that where I use the singular third-person pronoun, usually *he*, it is obvious that I imply the words *or she*.

judgmental of others, blaming the person who completed the suicide and finding fault with other grievers.

2. *The Helper*: the caring, interpersonal type. Demonstrative, generous, people-pleasing, and possessive. The helper focuses on the needs of others, sometimes to the detriment of his own needs. This type will likely be very concerned about what others think. Helpers will probably weave their grief into the grief of other people by wanting to help and care for the other grievers. A helper may have a deep sense of guilt because of feeling responsible for the suicide. In time, helpers will separate their personal grief from the grief of the people they help. At their lowest, they will be so focused on other people that they will neglect their own needs. As caregivers of suicide victims, helpers likely lose their own sense of value and may feel the suicide as an intense rejection.

3. *The Achiever*: the success-oriented, pragmatic type. Adaptive, excelling, driven, and image-conscious. The achiever has a need to be successful and not to fail. This type will likely grieve quickly and want to move on to other issues in life where he can be perceived as successful. Achievers may turn their grief into some kind of project they can accomplish. They may have special difficulties with the embarrassment and social stigma the suicide might cause them. In time, they will accept the suicide, and by their acceptance, help others to deal with the reality of the suicide. At their lowest, they may feel humiliated and become jealous of other grievers who they think are grieving better than they are. They may exhibit a lack of feelings.

4. *The Individualist*: the sensitive, withdrawn type. Expressive, dramatic, self-absorbed, and temperamental. The individualist wants to be special and unique, and has a need to understand his feelings and to avoid being ordinary. This type will probably identify and express feelings quite easily and symbolically.

Rituals, poetry, memorials, and pictures will be especially meaningful to individualists. They may find the suicide personally threatening. In time, they will probably transform the grief from the suicide into something personally valuable, dwelling on the positive memories of the deceased. At their lowest, they may become self-destructive, even suicidal themselves.

5. *The Observer*: the intense, cerebral type. Perceptive, secretive, and isolated. The observer (the thinker and investigator) tries to figure out the world and has a need to know and understand the universe, to be left alone, and to avoid looking foolish. This type will likely analyze the suicide, seeking details that will help understand the cause and nature of the suicide. An observer will find it helpful to connect this particular suicide with other suicides. Observers may find particular difficulty in the "why" of the suicide. In time, when they understand the motives that caused the suicide, they will find some consolation. At their lowest, they will withdraw from the family and society as much as they can. They may feel threatened, depressed, or overwhelmed by their grief when they are not able to understand it.

6. *The Loyalist*: the committed, security-conscious type. Engaging, responsible, anxious, and suspicious. The loyalist is committed to being faithful and dependable and has a need to receive approval and avoid being seen as rebellious. This type will probably seek the accepted ways to grieve a suicide through his faith tradition or society. Loyalists may be the first to seek help through a support group. They may have particular difficulties with feelings of abandonment. In time, they will trust their own feelings and also be supportive of other grievers. At their lowest, they will feel great insecurity, fear, and anxiety.

7. *The Adventurer*: the busy, fun-loving type. Spontaneous, versatile, distractible, and scattered. The adventurer (an enthusiast) is always on the go, seeking fun, and has a compulsive need to be happy and to avoid pain. This type will likely accept the suicide rather quickly and freely share his grief with others, seeking to incorporate this experience into his life. Adventurers may be especially receptive to mystical encounters with the deceased. In time, they will assimilate the suicide into their lives and achieve remarkable levels of acceptance. At their lowest, they may seek destructive ways to escape their grief, possibly through alcohol, drugs, or drastic changes in life style—anything to avoid the pain.

8. *The Leader*: the powerful, dominating type. Self-confident, decisive, willful, and confrontational. The leader (a challenger) is strong and in control, with a compulsive need to be self-reliant and to avoid being weak. This type will probably want to take charge of managing the practical matters following the suicide—funeral arrangements, estate settlement, etc. Leaders are inclined toward processing their grief quickly so they can prove to themselves and others that they are self-reliant and capable. They may have a particular problem accepting that they did not help prevent the suicide, if they feel they could have done something to stop it. Suicide causes them to have feelings of being betrayed. In time, their strength, guidance, and decision-making will reinforce other grievers and help them feel some stability. At their lowest, they may become dictatorial or aggressively demanding when others do not follow their directions. They are the last type to go to a support group.

9. *The Peacemaker*: the easygoing, self-effacing type. Receptive, agreeable, and complacent. The peacemaker tries to bring harmony into the world and has a compulsive need to keep the peace and to avoid conflict. This type will likely withdraw emotionally from the reality of the suicide in order to avoid

conflict. Internally, peacemakers will gradually accept the suicide as a necessary step toward their personal peace. They tend to seek a common ground among all the other grievers and to emphasize that commonality. In time, they will provide a comforting presence to others. At their lowest, they will withdraw from others, minimize the suicide, and refuse to accept any responsibility for relating to others or performing any tasks.

Any person may feel any of the emotions outlined in the nine personality types in the face of a suicide. But it is likely that each person will identify with the tendency of one of the types. When a person is able to identify with a personality type and its probable way of responding, that one has taken a large step in the direction of healing the grief suffered through the suicide of a loved one.

Look at the nine types and see which one seems to fit you the best. If you want to investigate the personality descriptions in greater detail, google the word *enneagram* to find out more about it.[16]

Understanding in general how other people grieve helps everyone cope with the aftermath of the suicide. Since people grieve differently and at their own pace, conflicts among suicide survivors are common. Using the enneagram as a tool for understanding these various approaches to this grief may minimize these conflicts and aid in the healing process not only of individuals, but also of a group of the family and friends of a loved one who completed suicide.

---

16   General descriptions of each type may be found on two websites. For more information about the enneagram, visit http://www.enneagraminstitute.com/Descript.asp and http://www.lessons4living.com/overview.htm.

Hope

The hope for suicide survivors, regardless of their personality type, their gender, or the emotions they experience, is that their future can be better than today. Of course, their lives will never be the same, but their "new normal" need not be dominated by their grief.

Following are some activities that have helped some suicide grievers.

- Reading this book or discussing these issues in a support group can help ease the pain.

- Talking with a counselor, friend, or even your deceased loved one can help you feel better.

- Visiting the grave site is a comfort for many people.

- Keeping a journal of your reactions and feelings provides relief and a release. Reading the journal some time later also lets you compare your current emotional state with what it was at an earlier time.

- Crying does help. Suicide tears wash away some of the grief, at least temporarily. Let yourself cry, men as well as women.

- Getting exercise is often essential to grief recovery; physical movement releases chemicals that counteract some depressive tendencies when we are so sad.

- Planting a tree or flowers as a memorial becomes a symbolic way to remember your loved one, which eliminates some portion of the loss.

All of these actions contribute to a better future and are acts of hope. The assurance here is that you can get to that point where you feel better emotionally than you may feel right now. At present, you may have to take this hope on faith in the people who have walked this terrible path before you and who care about you. Hope is personal and contagious. Look to others. It is not that they have "made it," but they are farther along than you are, and they give testimony and are personal witnesses that the future can be better than today.

If you can accurately identify and claim the emotions that you experience, and if you know yourself well enough to describe your personality correctly, you have some critical tools to help you through this tragic time. This journey to assimilation is not automatic, and without it, your life can be miserable and destructive for a long time. But through serious grief work, you do have legitimate hope for a more balanced future.

Questions for Personal Reflection or Group Discussion

1. To what extent is the suicide of your loved one an obvious suicide?

2. To what extent are you able to name your feelings that are associated with the suicide?

3. Describe in your own words what it means to "claim" your feelings.

4. Which of the twelve emotions outlined here are the ones that you experience most?

5. To what extent have your feelings changed since the death of your loved one?

6. To what extent have you experienced a difference in grief due to your gender?

7. Describe the enneagram in your own words.

8. Which of the nine personality types briefly introduced here seems to describe you the best?

9. To what extent does your grief experience match your personality type?

10. To what extent does this glance at different ways of grieving reflect your own experience and the experience of other family members and friends of your loved one who died by suicide?

11. How do you describe your hope that the future will be better than today?

CHAPTER 3

The Day They Died and All the Days Thereafter

The *When* Question

Monday, January 13, 2003, around 1:00 p.m.—that's when Karla shot herself—right after the holidays and the New Year. She visited us for Christmas and returned to Tulsa with Fran between Christmas and New Year. It was that cold and dreary time of the year, the beginning of that long spell of winter before spring finally arrives. Where we live in the St. Louis area it is a tedious time, when winter just hangs on interminably, when we can't play in the humid, chilling cold and snow like they do further north, and when we can't escape it without traveling south. With Karla's depression that year and then with her death (there were snow flurries when we buried her), 2003 was clearly the worst winter possible. Ever since, Christmas and New Year has had a cold shadow draped over it. After all, January 13 is not far behind.

On the other hand, there is no good time of the year for a suicide. Suicide survivors and veterans remember the day of the death with brutal clarity. Early grief magnifies the details of the suicide, how we reacted when we heard about it, and even more so for those who found the body. There may be initial shock, but we also remember the immediate impact of the tragedy; the shock does not erase that memory.

We know the date, the time, what we were doing when we heard, how we told others, how those first few hours went, what the first night was like, and how we reacted. It is one of the most memorable days of our lives, even beyond a wedding or the birth of our children. Regardless of the weather, time of year, morning or night, we remember. The day our loved one died is the day when loss was engraved on our souls. Our lives are changed forever.

A Suicide Time of the Year?

It is often assumed that suicides increase over the traditional holiday times of November and December. The theory is that those months include days and weeks that bring families and friends together in an atmosphere of joy, friendliness, and happy memories. The belief is that people who suffer from depression find it more difficult to cope with the expected positive emotions and as a result drift into a deeper depression and then take their own lives. The hectic schedules, gift buying, holiday expectations, and overall joyous atmosphere contribute to the decision to die by suicide.

The statistics do not verify this assumption. Suicides, in fact, are not more frequent during these holidays. Without denying the additional stress the holidays may create, this added anxiety does not lead to an unusual number of suicides.

It seems that the rates of suicide are the highest in the spring, followed by the summer months of June and July.[17]

Why there is a spike in suicides during these months is open to conjecture. Is it because April ushers in the spring with its promise of new life and warmth, which paradoxically highlights the depression? Is it because the increased outdoor activity of others emphasizes the gloom of depression? Is it because during the winter people are at home more, so there are more in-home interactions with people talking about their feelings who might be more inclined to help someone who is depressed? Is it because college is out? Is it because the warmer months promise more life, greater health, more positive possibilities and when these expectations are not met, a person with depression concludes that death is a better option than these unmet expectations?

Definitive answers to these questions are elusive. They are important questions for people who are attempting to prevent suicides. They are significant also to those who are trying to understand why a loved one died. Was the time of year a factor in the decision to end their lives? Another unanswered question. For those of us who are grieving the death of a loved one by suicide, it is too late to prevent it. Where our loved one ends up on the statistical scale of when people take their own lives is not relevant to our grief. We just know when they died.

Firsts

Immediately after the suicide, we begin a series of *firsts*: first days, first week, first month, first anniversary, first Thanksgiving, first spring, first … everything! Each "first" is a new experience, a hurdle. It seems impossible to cope with them, especially because we can't slow down time and do these "firsts" in slow motion.

17   Joiner, *Myths about Suicide*, 256f

They keep coming, ready or not! The accumulated impact of these unwanted firsts pile on us, stop us from thinking clearly, and bully us into a fatigue that sleep does not relieve, a weariness that does not recover, and a sadness that does not know how to smile. During these firsts it seems like the first is also the last in that these reactions seem permanent. They are not.

The first few days are crammed with practical details on top of the shock and initial grief. Funeral arrangements, obituary writing (do you include a reference to suicide or not?), insurance questions, travel plans for out-of-town family and friends, burial decisions, coffin selection, open or closed coffin, hundreds of practical decisions during a time when we are least capable of making those decisions. But we do it because we have to. During this time it is extremely valuable to have at least one person, preferably a few, to handle ordinary tasks: meals, cleaning, phone calls, company, organizing your time, and so forth. If there are people in your immediate circle of family and friends who are difficult for you, avoid them and stay close to the people who genuinely support you.

During these first few days you will have to decide what you tell people about the death. Some people are tempted to hide the suicide, to call it something else: an accident, a sudden heart attack, or something less painful to say. What do you say to children, for example? How do you tell an elderly and perhaps sickly grandparent?

Here are some things to consider as you try to decide what to say:

- Most suicide survivors and veterans will advise you to be honest and open about the death. To pretend it is something other than suicide adds to the emotional confusion, and it takes a lot of energy to keep the story straight in the future. Besides, you will worry about people discovering the truth, and you don't need this kind of additional anxiety as you try to deal with the emotional impact of the death.

- If people know about the suicide, they can offer you the kind of support you need.

- Even though some people may not know how to comfort you in the wake of the suicide, or know what to say to you, most people are accepting and try to understand your loss. They will be there for you in whatever way they can.

- You may not know what to say to them or even how you are "supposed" to respond. If you are confused, with conflicting emotions and muddled thinking, share your confusion.

It is better to be honest about the suicide rather than to try to hide it.

If you are hesitant about how to tell young children, seek advice from someone you trust. Go to a reputable website for suggestions, such as the one belonging to the American Foundation for Suicide Prevention.[18] You want to be the person who tells your children yourself, before they find out from someone else. It is often important to assure children that the suicide is not their fault.

As the weeks and months go by, you will likely feel many of the emotions described in chapter 2. What becomes clear is that there is no simple fix for this grief. You may feel better for a time, but then it hits hard again. Different people among your family and friends grieve differently, and it is hard to get everyone on the same page at the same time. These differences add to the sense of isolation and never-ending sadness.

Silence about the suicide is not grieving well. Some people believe that they must keep their loss within themselves, mainly because

---

18   The American Foundation for Suicide Prevention's website has this page to help with telling children about suicide: http://www.afsp.org/index. cfm?fuseaction=home.viewPage&page_id=FEDF6A4B-FA4D-F373-4F864EDAF1F49DC4.

that's the usual way they handle things. It is better to speak about it, to try to express your feelings. You may want to deal with things a little at a time, take one aspect of the pain, share that one piece, and then focus on another aspect. Little by little you can find more peace.

What often happens with suicide survivors, especially those who have lost other family members or friends to more conventional deaths, is that they begin grieving with the expectation that suicide grief will follow the pattern of other grief. Usually that doesn't happen. Suicide grief takes longer and feels different than grief following other deaths. It takes patience to accept this continuing grief. Time alone doesn't fix it, but time plus grief work will gradually change a survivor into a veteran.

During this time you may want to assure your family and friends that it is okay to talk about the suicide. Sometimes people feel that they don't want to bring it up to you because it may cause you more pain. Most of us *do* want to talk about it. It is actually more painful *not* to talk about it. Tell others it is generally fine to talk, and that you will let them know if you are not up to it at this point. Just be honest about it, but lean more toward talking than not talking. Talk until you don't have to talk any more. You may repeat yourself, retell the story of what happened, and talk about how you are thinking. It is okay to repeat it, even to the same people. They need to know that you need to say it out loud often in order to face the reality.

Some survivors during these early weeks and months say that they "feel the presence" of their loved one, either in dreams or under certain circumstances. These survivors usually report these feelings as a great comfort. If you do not have these experiences, it is not a sign that you didn't love enough or aren't sensitive enough now. Such experiences are not a measure of your love or the quality of the relationship you had with your loved one.

While you may be depressed, anxious, confused, or angry, it remains important that you take care of yourself. If you cannot sleep enough, talk to your doctor about possible medication to help you sleep. Get regular exercise. Walk, run, go to the gym, use a treadmill, play basketball, tennis, or golf (and walk the course!)—whatever you need to do to keep moving and physically active. The temptation is to just sit, stare, and cry. Some of that may be inevitable, but after you do it for a while, get up and walk a few miles. Keeping physically active is a critical part of your grief work. Don't shortchange that activity or yourself.

The First Anniversary

As you approach the first anniversary of the suicide, you will likely feel an increase in your grief. This upsurge is normal and expected. The anniversary is an especially tough time because it brings back many of the emotions of a year ago. Part of it may be that you thought that by now you wouldn't feel so bad. Chances are the grief remains stronger than you anticipated or hoped. Grief recovery doesn't happen in a straight line, always gradually getting better. It comes and goes, two steps forward and one step back. The time between especially bad grief episodes does get longer, but the coming of the first anniversary generally moves us into a deeper grief phase.

Some survivors maintain that the anticipation of the first anniversary is worse than the day itself. Others say that the anniversary day was terrible. It is a good idea to plan the day: Will it be a routine day? Will you take off work? Will you have a gathering of family and friends to remember your loved one? Do you prefer to be alone, or with just a few people? Will there be some kind of ritual? Candle? Photos? Telling stories about your loved one? Music? Perhaps write a letter to your loved one and read it out loud? Make a special meal? Plant a tree? Host a prayer service? Create a website? Make a donation? Buy a memorial ad in the newspaper? Call family or friends who live at a distance?

There are many options for the first anniversary. If the day meets your expectations, you may want to adapt it for future anniversaries. On the Sunday nearest Karla's anniversary we invite family and a few friends to our church service, followed by a brunch at which we ask everyone to share a memory of Karla. Over the years these memories are more about how Karla lived, rather than how she died. That's a perspective we have all found helpful.

Whatever you decide, do something on the anniversary. Otherwise the day may arrive and the grief may be devastating. The occasion also provides a unique opportunity to honor your loved one and for participants to commend each other on making it through the first year. It is clearly not the end to the grief journey, but it is a milestone. It is also an opportune time to look back three months, six months, and nine months to track how your grief has changed over the year. In some ways, the pain may be as intense as it was that first week. In other ways, it may be less intense. In any case, it will be different, and it is helpful to identify those differences and to talk about them.

The Grief Calendar

The first anniversary of the suicide is often the hardest calendar date to face. But there are others. Many of our holidays are woven into the fabric of our family life, and they often become reminders of our loss. Suicide is different from other losses, as we noted. The grief is harder and longer, so the calendar dates of holidays and holy days are also harder. The next few pages of this *when* chapter follow the calendar year and offer some comments that may apply to the grief of some survivors. Some of these days will likely be more difficult for some survivors; other dates may affect other people. Some holidays may not apply to everyone, but often these dates are problematic, and they provide a convenient format to address various aspects of suicide grief.

New Year's Day

The new year begins with parties, resolutions, a turn of the page, and an expectation of hope. People who struggle with suicide grief cannot enter into the joyous spirit of a hopeful future. Someone is missing who should be there, who decided not to see another new year. The optimism of a new year loses to the sadness of the grief.

In the early experience of suicide grief, the grief controls the survivor. Thinking, feeling, and acting are all fueled by the loss. We feel powerless. Resolutions and looking forward to the future are impossible. Grief dominates. Not much else matters. We may go through the motions of our routine life, but there is nothing routine about it.

It is probably best to skip New Year celebrations during this early grief period. Sleep out the old and sleep in the new. What difference does it make if there is a new year on the calendar? In the greater scheme of things, maybe next year you can enter into some of the expected spirit of a calendar change. Then again, maybe not.

Expectations about how you are supposed to feel and act because it's a new year do not apply to you. Do what feels right to you. In a family, one person may want to try to celebrate, while someone else in the family simply can't do it. Respect each other's position, and agree on how you are going to work it out. But in no case should one person force another griever to experience New Year in a way that is not comfortable. Work it out with love and respect.

Valentine's Day

Valentine's Day is more than a marketing program for Hallmark. It is one day our society puts a premium on love. For suicide survivors and veterans it raises a perplexing question: Why wasn't my love enough to prevent the suicide of my loved one?

It is a haunting question, and at least for me, once it is asked and answered, it is asked again because my answer isn't completely satisfying. I know that I loved Karla and I tried to show that love in the best way that I knew. But it didn't keep her alive. If I could have her back, would I love her more or better or differently so that she wouldn't take her life? I would try but I know that I have no control over the end result. I wish it were otherwise.

If love were enough to prevent suicide, there would be far fewer suicides. It may take time, study, counseling, and reflection, but the truth is our love does not control anyone else. The other person can reject it, ignore it, and choose someone or something else. All we can do is express our love as best we can in the way our personality allows us. Whether the other person accepts our love depends on the other person because love is limited by the loved one.

In the case of Karla, I believe she knew we loved her—that many people loved her. But her depression was stronger. At that moment, she was convinced that her hopelessness was permanent, that she didn't belong, and that she was a burden to all of us and to the world. It's likely that she thought she was doing the best thing for us, by leaving our lives. She was dead wrong, of course. But I am convinced that that's how she thought and felt.

I also believe that many people who take their own lives feel like Karla did, and that many survivors feel like I did and do. Love does not conquer all. It never has, and it never will. It is not love's purpose to conquer. It is love's purpose to stand with, understand, respect, forgive, and care. It is not love's purpose or ability to force itself on someone else. Valentine's Day is wonderful and needed. But it doesn't understand survivors or, in the final analysis, love itself.

Easter and Passover

Jews celebrate Passover and Christians celebrate Easter around the same time of the year. They always occur in March or April. The religious feasts and the seasonal change point to new life. In these holy days, as in nature itself, there is a renewal of life.

Suicide survivors early in their grief journey see no possibility of a renewed life for themselves. They often feel like they will never be happy again. The religious liturgical cycles and the cycle of nature can't penetrate the grief. There is only painful loss. Our personal calendar does not match the external calendar of feasts and nature.

But Easter, Passover, and spring are important reminders that our deepest grief need not be permanent. Even for us in our personal, painful journey, there is resurrection, the promised land, and warmer weather. We need to hear the rest of the story even when we can barely hear anything positive. Other people get through the toughest part of suicide grief, and so can we. We don't know how at this point, and we don't see an end to the worst, but it does happen. That's why it is extremely valuable to talk with survivors who are further along on the journey to becoming veterans. That's why support groups for suicide survivors are so crucial. That's why grief work is priceless. That's why trusting in a better future is critical. That's why hope remains real. It does get better, just like Jews believe in the Passover experience and Christians proclaim a resurrection, and everyone experiences a spring. Devastating grief does not have to win. Believe that and you are on your way to a better tomorrow and a manageable form of grief.

Mother's Day

For mothers who lost a child to suicide or children who lost a mother to suicide, this annual celebration may add another layer of grief, especially in the first few years after the death. While everyone else is focusing on positive thoughts about mothers, these survivors grieve the loss of their mothers, or mothers of their children. The social buildup to the day highlights the loss as these grievers wonder why their mothers no longer wanted to be mothers, or why their children no longer wanted mothers.

It isn't true in every family, but often the mother figure is the emotional glue of the family. The mother nurtures the child. The mother or child who dies by suicide breaks and rejects that nurturing relationship. Thoughts like these can magnify the grief and create a detour on the path to grief recovery.

Father's Day

A similar comment can be made about Father's Day. This day may be more difficult for men; for the most part, men in our society are expected to control their emotions and to be more reserved than women in expressing their feelings. Men are supposed to face tragedies with strength, discipline, and the innate ability to overcome the emotions that normally follow the suicide of a loved one.

Crying in public; inability to work due to grief; having difficulty "getting on with their lives"; needing professional help to cope with their grief; inability to prevent the suicide; not thinking clearly; inability to compartmentalize the grief and thereby control it—all of these reactions common to suicide survivors run contrary to the societal expectations of manliness. A male who is grieving the suicide of a loved one may experience the intensity of these feelings for the first time and may not have the emotional experience to cope with them successfully.

Father's Day may be the occasion when this aspect of suicide grief emerges.

Independence Day

The Fourth of July may not be an especially tough day for most suicide survivors. But it was a big day for Karla. Therefore, in our family, each Independence Day is a special reminder of her. As a kid, she always loved the "boom-booms." The term and the celebration stayed with her until she died. Each year the "boom-booms" bring back memories of her.

The first few years, when we were primarily suicide survivors, these memories were very painful as we focused on her death and our loss. In more recent years, as we transitioned into suicide veterans, the Fourth of July now brings back more positive memories of her joy in watching and participating in the fireworks and festivities. I still have visions of her lying on a blanket on the warm summer night and looking up to the sky, reveling in the colors and sounds of a rousing fireworks display, especially with the *1812 Overture* playing during the bombastic and glorious finale.

I mention it here because there may be a special holiday, not necessarily Independence Day—perhaps Memorial Day or Veterans Day—that had particular significance for your loved one. If that is the case, my hope for you is that those memories can transition from painful to agreeable, and then perhaps to pleasant.

Labor Day

I single out Labor Day in this grief calendar to remind us that grief is work—a lot of work. In fact, it may be the hardest work you have ever done because it is so deep, so personal, and so shattering. Most people simply don't recover from this grief without the honest, brutal, and thorough emotional labor that is necessary to become a genuine suicide grief veteran. Often tears, confusion, emotional turmoil, perseverance, patience, and dogged determination are required to go from initial devastation to manageable assimilation. That is work with a capital *W*.

It is possible to travel this journey to assimilation. But it does take work. What kind of work? Emotional work; psychological labor; believing that things can get better; humility to seek help; avoiding the temptation to try to ignore our pain; letting go of the impulse to just move on without acknowledging the hurt. It is hard work. And we have no experience to rely on, nothing that prepares us for this kind of loss. Labor Day is truly our day.

Thanksgiving

It's hard to be thankful when we are grieving a suicide. What is there to be thankful for? We can list the things and people for whom we should be thankful, but that list doesn't measure up to the list with one name on it. All the thank-yous sound hollow. And by the way—skip the turkey and the trimmings. None of it tastes right anyway. And who cares who wins what football game? Not all Thanksgivings need to be that bleak, but some of them may very well be.

On the other hand, we should make that gratitude list. Even the physical exercise of creating the list insists that there are other parts of life besides the suicide. Regardless of how much celebrating we do during the Thanksgiving weekend, it is important to recall that we are grateful for other family members, for things we right now take for granted and that are in the background of our life because the suicide has absorbed all of our immediate focus.

For our first Thanksgiving after Karla died, we accepted an invitation from Fran's sister who lives in Milwaukee to join her family for Thanksgiving. That was the right decision. And we talked about Karla around the Thanksgiving table. That, too, was the right decision.

Christmas and Hanukkah

The year ends with perhaps the most challenging season for suicide grievers. The season of Christmas and Hanukkah is so long, the hype is so intense, the expectations are so high, the joy is so pervasive, the spirit is so positive, the music is so festive, and the religious feasts are so dramatic that suicide grievers are often numb and overwhelmed by it all. It is hectic enough without the suicide, even though there are emotional and spiritual payoffs during these days. With the suicide, what used to be payoffs are now painful memories that rip the soul out of the celebrations.

But Christmas and Hanukkah happen whether we want them to or not, and whether we are ready or not. It might be helpful to ask: Would our loved ones want us to avoid participating in the holiday celebrations? No, they would not. They didn't want us to grieve through the holidays or to suffer. They did not die to punish us or hurt us. They did not wish us pain. They mistakenly thought they were freeing us from the burden they caused us. It clearly will not take away all the sorrow we especially feel around these holidays; but remembering their intentions when they died provides a context and perspective that could help us get through the end of the year with less pain.

Besides, in time and with grief work, it does get better.

Coping with the Grief Calendar

Here are a few ideas that may be helpful as you try to cope with the grief calendar:

1. It is okay not to celebrate one or many of the days on your grief calendar. It is okay to skip traditions. It is okay to eat a simple, ordinary meal and do nothing. It is okay to be alone or with just a few comfortable friends. It is also okay to join a large group who will do what you have always done on a special day. It is okay to laugh and to tell stories and to root for your favorite team. It is all okay. The point is that you decide how you want to spend these holidays.

   In order to spend it in the way you want, you will have to make a plan and think it through with your family. Don't let it sneak up on you and try to figure it out that day. Think about it. But don't accept any pressure about what you are expected to do or not do; don't perform tasks that you don't freely choose to do; don't visit with any people that you don't want to be around. Do it the way you want to do it, and if it doesn't work out like you thought it would, or it isn't as bad as you felt it might be, that's okay too.

   If this pattern is necessary for two, three, four, or more years, guess what? That's okay too. Suicide grief is life altering, and adjusting a life after this death may take some time and reflection. Each year you will likely feel a little differently about your grief calendar events.

2. If you are in a family setting, and different people have different ways they want to deal with the day, work it out among you honestly. There may be a need for some compromises. Just do the adjusting kindly and with respect for everyone's feelings.

   Fran and I have often used a system of determining what is important to us. It is a simple *one-two-three* system. A *one* means this event, or part of an event, is very important. A *two* means it is something I would like, but less important than a one. And a *three* means I would prefer it, but it is no big deal if I don't do it. Then we tell each other what number we label the event or part of the event with. If she feels it is a one and I feel it is two or three, then we go with the one. If we both think it is a one but we have opposite opinions, we then have to discuss it further. It is a system that has worked for us in many situations. And it might be useful if there are differences regarding how you want to deal with one of the days on your grief calendar.

3. Some survivors say that the anticipation of an anniversary, birthday, or holiday is worse than the day itself.

4. It is usually meaningful to create some ritual for some of the days on your calendar. The use of a designated candle with some sharing time about your loved one seems to be the most common ritual. Displaying pictures or symbols may be a good idea. Perhaps a favorite reading would be appropriate. It seems best to do this ritual at the beginning of the gathering since the suicide is on everyone's mind anyway.

5. What you do one year does not have to be the same in following years. Do only what is meaningful for your family. In time, you will have a pattern that works for you.

6. If you belong to a faith community, you may want to establish an ongoing remembrance of your loved one with that community through prayer, ritual, or a memorial of some kind.

Those are some ideas on how to cope with your grief calendar. You can also create your own ways of dealing with these days, relying on your knowledge of your loved one, your ethnic and cultural background, your lifestyle, your interests, and your personality. Your object should be to capture the spirit of your loved one's life, not just the death, and to express that spirit in a way that is meaningful to you.

This planning is meant to counteract the temptation to ignore your loved one in the mistaken belief that ignoring will minimize the loss and accelerate the process of "getting on with your life." That attitude undermines the value of your loved one and sabotages your grief. For your sake, the sake of your loved one, and the sake of everyone around you, don't let this negative attitude interfere with your progress from survivor to veteran. You and everyone else around you deserve better.

Grieving the Future

Suicide grief, especially when the person who dies is younger, is not only about past memories and present pain. It is also about the future, a future that will not be as we thought it would be. Any death of a younger person raises a similar, future-oriented grief, but the presumed semi-deliberate death by suicide makes the grief more complicated and harder.

The *when* of suicide grief involves all dimensions of any timeline. What would have been becomes a haunting echo of the grief. Our loved one does not have a future; he (or she) died by his own hand. We had some expectations of a future with him and for him. The specifics of those expectations vary from person to person, but the loss of their future revises our future as well. We have concrete images of the past—photos, letters, mementos, documentation, and so forth—which anchor our grief that centers on the past. We have our current emotions and events that anchor our present grief. But our grief for the future that will not be is unanchored and open to our imagination, projections, and possibilities. Was there a marriage in the future? Might there have been children, jobs, accomplishments, relationships, turmoil, disappointments, joy, or suffering? All these possibilities complicate our grief because all we know with certainty is that there is no future for our loved one. If we believe in an afterlife, how do we imagine that?

Grieving the future is a large part of our grief, and it isn't always identified as such. We may miss this future dimension by our strong focus on the past and the present. It is helpful to spend some time reflecting upon and discussing this future orientation to our grief. To name it accurately, as we saw in chapter two, is extremely valuable as we cope with our grief. Clarify your unfulfilled dreams of the future, face them, and gently discard them. That process is critical on your journey to assimilation, going from survivor to veteran.

Age-Related Suicides

Another dimension to the *when* question revolves around the age of people who die by suicide. The statistics tell us that in 2010, 12.4 of every 100,000 Americans died by suicide, one every 13.7 minutes. That's a total of 38,364 people. But at what age do these people die? Suicides are not evenly distributed over all age groups.

There is more risk for suicide among the elderly and the young than for the vast majority of people who are between the ages of twenty-four and sixty-five.

A statistic that may surprise you is that elderly adults have rates of suicide close to 50 percent higher than that of all other ages. Men over seventy kill themselves at a rate higher than any other demographic. White men over eighty-five are at the greatest risk of all age-gender-race groups. Does your loved one fit in this older person category? Before Karla died and I began this kind of research, I had no idea that suicide was this prevalent among older people. My guess is that many of these suicides are recorded as "old age" or some other physical cause of death so survivors don't have to deal with the pain of suicide grief. I can't prove that observation, but it sounds plausible. A coroner I know has made the same observation. To the extent that it is accurate, it demonstrates how much we fear and want to avoid this kind of grief. Honestly, it makes sense to me. Would I prefer to hear that my great-grandfather died by suicide at age eighty-seven, or that he died of "old age"? I would choose old age.

One of the leading causes of suicide among the elderly is depression, often undiagnosed or untreated. The act of completing suicide is rarely preceded by only one cause or one reason. In the elderly, common risk factors include

- the recent death of a loved one;
- a previous suicide attempt;
- physical illness, uncontrollable pain, or the fear of a prolonged illness;
- perceived poor health;
- social isolation and loneliness;
- the presence of a mental illness;
- major changes in social roles (such as retirement).

On the other end of the age spectrum, youths (ages fifteen to twenty-four) also have elevated rates of suicide. In 2010, suicide ranked as the third-leading cause of death for young people (ages fifteen to twenty-four); only accidents and homicides occurred more frequently.

In the past sixty years, the suicide rate has quadrupled for males fifteen to twenty-four years old, and has doubled for females of the same age. Each day there are approximately 10.5 youth suicides. The young were 14.1 percent of the 2010 population and comprised 12.0 percent of the suicides. Every two hours and seven minutes, a person under the age of twenty-five completes suicide.

Research has shown that most adolescent suicides occur after school hours and in the teen's home. Most adolescent suicide attempts are precipitated by interpersonal conflicts. The intent of the behavior appears to be to effect change in the behaviors or attitudes of others.

It is estimated that there are more than 1,100 suicides on college campuses per year. One in twelve college students have made a suicide plan. Of the students who had seriously considered suicide, 94.8 percent reported feeling so sad to the point of not functioning at least once in the past year, and 94.4 percent reported feelings of hopelessness. Two groups of students might be at higher risk for suicide: students with a preexisting (before college) mental health condition, and students who develop a mental health condition while in college.

That's a lot of numbers and statistics; and they are impersonal, removed from our grief. But they indicate something real about the deaths of our loved ones if they fit the elderly or youth categories. Sometimes there is comfort in numbers; knowing that our loved one is not the only person to die by suicide may be somewhat comforting. Acknowledging that he or she is part of an age group with elevated suicides may offer some consolation, even though the personal grief is clearly tied to your personal situation.[19]

Hope

After a suicide, when do we become hopeful? The initial shock and other intense emotions are so all-consuming that hope is not even in the picture. Hope is the conviction that the future will be better than the present, but the first few weeks and months

---

19   These statistics were gathered from the National Center for Injury Prevention and Control (NCIPC) website operated by the Centers for Disease Control and Prevention (CDC) at http://www.cdc.gov/ncipc/wisqars/default.htm.

after the suicide, we generally don't see a better future. The grief overwhelms the hope.

But hope can emerge. If you believe in an afterlife, the hope for our loved ones revolves around the conviction that they are in a better place, a state where their illness or impulse to end their lives no longer prevails. Their suffering is over. If you do not believe in an afterlife, your hope may center on the fact that they will suffer no more, that the life they perceived as painful and hopeless is over. Life, you may believe, was a frightening and bleak experience for them. And they thought it would never get better. You may even agree with them. They have ended their pain.

If your loved one died in what appears to be a random, impulsive act, then your hope for that one can be based on the life he lived prior to death. A tragic impulse does not erase someone's previous life.

In the initial days of my grief, I felt that Karla was now at peace, but I wasn't. Hope for us survivors slowly emerges from our grief. With grief work and in time, we gradually bring the death into balance with the rest of our life. We become familiar with the feeling of loss, and what is familiar becomes more manageable. We assimilate the suicide in with other events and relationships. The future becomes now, and we feel better. Obviously, the suicide always retains a major impact on our lives, but other people, other responsibilities, and other events crowd out the grief, shrinking it to a size that we can usually handle. And that experience fuels the hope that the future can be better.

Questions for Personal Reflection or Group Discussion

1. When did your loved one die? What were you doing when you heard about it? What was your initial reaction?

2. Describe your first weeks after the suicide. What was the funeral like? How did you deal with the practical details? Who was most supportive to you during this period?

3. Describe the rest of the first year after the death. What happened on the first anniversary?

4. Which days on your grief calendar did you find most difficult? Why?

5. Which days on your grief calendar seemed to be easier? Why?

6. Which of the coping strategies associated with your grief calendar do you find most helpful?

7. What other ways not mentioned in the text do you use to cope with your grief calendar?

8. How well do you cope with the future that will never be because of the suicide? Describe some of the events or expectations you had that died when he or she died.

9. If your loved one fit either the elderly or youth suicide profile, how do you respond to that aspect of the death?

10. To what extent are you hopeful about the future of your loved one and about your future as a suicide survivor or veteran?

CHAPTER 4

Does It Matter Where They Died?

The *Where* Question

Yes, it matters.

Knowing the place, the surroundings, and the circumstances of a suicide is important to most survivors. We want to picture what happened as we ask why it happened. The location of the death provides a concrete setting for the picture. We sometimes ask: If our loved ones had been somewhere else, in different surroundings, would they have completed the suicide? Would a different location have prevented the death? More permanently unanswerable questions.

Karla died in a small, light blue, cinder block bedroom that was part of a makeshift living area in a vending machine repair shop in the west end of Tulsa, Oklahoma. It was in an old warehouse area of the city, on the industrialized west side of the Arkansas River, which runs through Tulsa. She was there the morning of

January 13, 2003, because Lonnie, a friend of hers, lived there as a guard protecting the repair shop, which is owned by his father. Lonnie is a kind man, older than Karla, who shared with her similar ideas on history, philosophy, theology, and depression. She simply was where he was on that fateful Monday afternoon, three days after she was released from a behavioral treatment center. He left earlier that day to do some chores and found her body when he returned.

While that small bedroom didn't cause her to find the hidden gun that killed her, it is the place where she died. It is, then, a decisive place in her life—and therefore also in our lives. A week after she died, Fran and I, with our friend Ginny, drove to Tulsa to sell her old car, close out her room in Madonna House where she lived, sort through her clothes, and visit with a few of her friends, including Lonnie.

And then there was the time I spent in that tiny bedroom. I wanted to connect with that place emotionally. It's where my daughter took her last breath as she pulled the trigger. It's where her desperation and pain reached down into her being and convinced her that dying would end the torment. I wanted the walls and floor and ceiling to shout that they tried to stop her and then to whisper into my heart that she was now at peace. The place of her death transported me back to the place of her birth and her first breath. I was there in the operating room of St. Joseph Hospital in Ottumwa, Iowa, when she arrived ten minutes after Kevin, at 7:40 in the morning of August 7, 1976. Those two rooms anchored her life.

I need to know how those two rooms are connected, beyond the obvious fact that everyone has to be born someplace and everyone has to die someplace. Karla's first room spoke of life, joy, possibilities, and wonder, while her last room cried from desperation, pain, hopelessness, and death. In between those two rooms, every place she went bore her footprint and her spirit.

To this day, places she touched still touch me. But those two contradictory rooms speak louder to me than many of the other places she graced. Those walls contain the extremes of her life and her death. Did the first room draw a map to the last room? Was there something in her baby genes that pointed to her last act? If so, did I generate that gene? Or did the many places she traveled to and lived in during her twenty-six years add to her need to end her life in that small, cinder block bedroom? Still more unanswerable questions.

What I do know is that her life and her death are intertwined. Her final act of desperation is not separated from the rest of her life. What began in a hospital room in 1976 is the beginning of a continuum that continues today, through her death, and is still going strong. The death room in Tulsa does not erase her past or our future. Those places contained her life and death, and absorbed her spirit, received her, and still bear her mark. For a few moments, standing in her last room, I felt that connection with her life and her despair. It was a sacred time in a sacred place. It will always be so.

My guess is that other survivors have similar feelings about the place where their loved one died.

On the Other Hand …

Some survivors may not relate emotionally to the place where their loved one died. Outside of an immediate interest in the circumstances of the death, these grievers may focus so much on why they died, how they died, and their own grief, that the place of the suicide seems insignificant. That perspective is understandable. The suicide grief journey can take many turns, and no one can follow all the same paths at the same time.

At some point in the grieving process, however, it is helpful for survivors to center on the place their loved one died. My hope is that all survivors will eventually become veterans, and that the deaths of loved ones they experience will be assimilated into their lives. Coming to some level of comfort with the place of the death is a part of the assimilation process. That place contains the awful reality of the suicide. Remembering that place—or imagining that place, if you cannot visit there—and coping with the brutal truth contained in that place may be the final obstacle to assimilation.

Some survivors cannot bear to think about "that place" because doing so feels like a terrifying nightmare. If that is someone's initial reaction to the place where their loved one died, my suggestion is not to force the assimilation. But at a later time, when it is possible to visualize or visit the site, I suggest that every survivor make that visit or visualize the place. It is the place where your loved one released the pain that drove him to suicide, and in that sense, it is the place of his transition from agony to peace. For each of us, it is a place of tragedy. But a conversion is also possible for survivors, and the place of death can be a place of solace, acceptance, peace, and assimilation for us. That transition is not automatic or assured, but confronting this place directly is crucial for some suicide survivors in order to become veterans.

Do not confront this terrible place by running from it or ignoring it, but by letting those final moments of your loved one's life enter you in order to leave you. Allow that place to reside temporarily in your heart, to touch you as you touch the walls and whatever was there at the time of death. Making emotional contact with the place connects one with the reality of the death. Moving from survivor to veteran includes confronting the fact of suicide. No one can effectively go around, over, or under that central, devastating truth as much as he might want or try to. Facing it means facing that place.

Where in the Country

There are states and regions in the United States where suicide rates are significantly higher than average. The American Association of Suicidology found in the year 2010 that Wyoming had the highest rate of suicide (23.2 per 100,000 population), and the District of Columbia had the lowest rate (6.8). The national average rate is 12.4 per state. The top eleven states are from the Western region: Wyoming, Alaska, Montana, Nevada, New Mexico, Idaho, Oregon, Colorado, South Dakota, Utah, and Arizona.

The areas with the lowest rates of suicide are the District of Columbia, New York, New Jersey, Maryland, Massachusetts, Illinois, Connecticut, California, Nebraska, and Minnesota, in that order. All of these 2010 rankings are similar to previous years.[20]

The Golden Gate Bridge, the iconic landmark of San Francisco, is the world's most frequently chosen suicide site. Since its construction in 1937, more than 1,500 people have jumped from that bridge and died. The Aokigahara forest, Mount Fuji, Japan, claims up to seventy-eight suicides a year and is thought to be the second most often selected suicide location in the world.

There appears to be some significance to where a person lives that enters into the reasons why people take their lives. The difference between the highest rates (23.2) and the lowest (6.8) is substantial. But it is not clear why there is such a wide and consistent gap between states and regions.

Is it because some states are more active in suicide prevention? Is it because the western region has more remote territory, which means people live in more isolated areas? Is it because mental

---

20   J. L. McIntosh and C. W. Drapeau, "U.S.A. suicide 2010: Official final data" (Washington, DC: American Association of Suicidology, 2012), http://www. suicidology.org.

health services are less available in some states than in others? Is it because more people have greater access to firearms in some parts of the country than in other parts? Is it because some states have more of a culture of "honor code" than other areas? Is there an ethnic aspect to suicide to such an extent that regions that are heavily populated with a specific ethnic group will have higher rates of suicide than other areas without that ethnic presence? Is it because the average age of people in some regions better fits the profile of potential suicides? Is suicide more likely in rural areas than in urban areas? Is suicide more prevalent in regions of greater poverty?

All these are questions without definitive answers. Most of the research about suicide centers on the *why* of the act, not the *where*. For suicide survivors and veterans, the *where* of the suicide in terms of the state or region is a past event. It clearly does not explain the key question of why our loved ones took their lives, but it may add a small piece to the puzzle for some survivors.

Where They Died

There is another question regarding where they died. Did they die at home or elsewhere? The answer has a much greater impact on the survivors than the question of where in the country they might have died.

Karla died in Tulsa, four hundred miles away from Shiloh, Illinois, where we live. Kevin was living in St. Louis at the time, and was on a work assignment in Milwaukee on January 13, 2003, the day Karla died. For those of us who were far away at the time of the suicide and could not arrive on the scene in a reasonable time, the distance added to the initial shock and loss. The tendency is to want to be there, to go there when something like this happens. The physical closeness feels like a form of connectedness with our loved one. To be there reinforces our love and verifies our loss.

It's not that I didn't believe the Shiloh police officer who told me, "Karla Smith has died." That's all he knew. I immediately said, "She killed herself." He was surprised that I jumped to that conclusion, but of course he knew nothing of her history. At that moment I wanted to be in Tulsa, to be involved in the immediate aftermath of her death, to do something with her, for her, around her. I wanted to be there, not four hundred miles away. I doubt there was anything I could have done; I just wanted to be there.

I told Fran when she came home from work a few minutes later. Eventually I got Kevin on the phone and told him. Our pastor came over, and my sisters and some friends joined us that night. We sat, we mourned together, we prayed. We quietly remembered her. We tried to be practical and figure out what to do next. But mainly we cried, sobbed, wailed, and went numb. But we weren't there. And Kevin was in Milwaukee.

I don't know if it is "better" to be there after the suicide or "better" to be miles away. Every suicide experience is unique, with some common features, and all survivors have to deal with the particulars of their situation. It is not helpful to compare my experience with Karla with someone else's experience of suicide in terms of which one is worse, or harder, or more complicated. Is it more difficult to grieve the suicide of a young person or a senior citizen? Is it easier to accept the suicide of someone who is dying of cancer, or a person who has suffered from clinical depression for decades? Is it less painful to cope with the suicide of a single man or with the mother of three young children? And, once again, is it better to be there or to be miles away?

Making these kinds of comparisons complicates the grieving. Each situation has its own story, with a unique combination of personalities, relationships, and history. To grieve effectively we need to deal with the specific combination that evolves from each suicide. We listen to other stories, not to compare theirs with ours, but to find points of contact, courage, and helpful insights; also to share—but not compare—our stories, memories, hopes, pain, comfort, struggles, understanding, and our strength. No suicide is harder or better than another. That reality applies to all aspects of the death including the *where* of the suicide.

Dying at Home

When the suicide happens at home, the surviving family members must contend with seeing the place of the death on a regular basis. That constant contact with the specific site of the suicide adds another dimension to the grief process. If the suicide was in the basement, some survivors avoid going "down there" as much as possible. If the death took place in a bedroom, some survivors don't go into that room for a long time. If the place of the suicide was a common room, like the kitchen or living room, survivors sometimes redecorate the room or change things around in order to avoid reinforcing the picture of the death they carry in their minds. In some cases, the survivors sell the home and move to a different place in order to escape the constant reminder of the death.

All of these reactions to the death are okay. Survivors must do what they have to do in order to cope with their loss. Of course, it is better to talk about personal feelings with other trusted people and not to make impulsive decisions that might seem right at the moment but which may have negative consequences down the road. Some people advise us not to make major decisions (move to a different location, change jobs, get remarried if a spouse died, quit school, and so on) during the first year after such a tragic loss. That seems like sound advice to me, but each survivor must make these decisions based on his own situation. That is why it is so important to seek guidance from trusted personal friends and professionals. Impulsive decisions generally lead to more complications than solutions.

The Need for a Counselor

In all of these situations, whether the death is at home or at a distance, it may be necessary to see a professional counselor. We are very vulnerable for quite some time after the death, and our emotions may affect our thinking to such an extent that we would be better off talking about our grief with someone who knows how to help us identify what's going on within us and who can guide us through the grief journey. Many survivors find a counselor or a support group and testify to the value of this kind of help.

I did not see a professional counselor after Karla died, but I did visit regularly with Father Bill Hitpas, my pastor, who has also been a good friend since high school. He actually served as my counselor, and has the requisite skills to an exceptional degree. I am still grateful for those valuable conversations, often over lunch.

At this point, I consider myself a suicide veteran, but my journey through the toughest part of the grief is a path that many other survivors might not take. I read extensively after Karla died, and I wrote a journal, which helped me focus my feelings. I also traveled by car a lot at that time, and I took along a recorder, which gave me the chance to talk out loud while I was driving and to listen back to what I was saying. Since I am also a writer, I wrote a book on our family experience with bipolar disorder and suicide titled *The Tattered Tapestry: A Family's Search for Peace with Bipolar Disorder.*[21] The journaling helped me focus on my personal feelings, and the book helped me transfer some of those experiences to my readers.

Reading and writing, then, were helpful tools for my personal grief journey. Talking and sharing life with my family and friends was also very comforting. I made some mistakes during this journey, but by and large I feel like I have been through the

---

21   Published by iUniverse, 2005.

worst of the grief and am now usually at the state of assimilation, though with periodic and sometimes unpredictable lapses back into some of the more negative and depressive emotions associated with suicide grief.

The other part of my journey that contributes to assimilation is our decision to create and our continuing work with our family foundation, the *Karla Smith Foundation* (KSF). Our intention is to follow Karla's lead in educating and supporting people with mental health problems. The mission of KSF is "to provide hope for a balanced life to the family and friends of anyone with mental illness or who lost a loved one to suicide." We offer support groups, awareness events, educational conferences, and presentations, and we collaborate with many organizations in the effort to reduce stigma and address the multiple needs related to mental illness and suicide. Visit our website for more information at www. KarlaSmithFoundation.org.

Even though I am now retired, I work many hours on programs and issues related to KSF. Given my personality, this work also helps me personally deal with the loss of Karla. I acknowledge her death, but I believe KSF keeps her spirit alive while it helps other people.

In any case, I repeat my suggestion to see a professional grief counselor, minister, or therapist. Many people in our support group for suicide grievers testify to the value of talking with a therapist or counselor. If you do see a counselor, one of the issues you will likely want to discuss is this current question of where your loved one died, at home or at a distance.

Grieving in Public

Expressions of grief happen anywhere. Sometimes they are predictable, such as when visiting the cemetery. Standing there looking at the marker often leads to tears, or even worse, sadness without tears. In the first year or two after her death, talking about Karla's suicide in public often led to crying, something I was not accustomed to or comfortable with. But in time I could cry in public without any concern. I finally came to the conviction that if anyone else had a problem with me crying in public, it was their problem, not mine. I had enough to deal with on my own. And what I discovered is that most people do not have an issue with public tears. As a result, my public crying, and others' reaction to it, made it easier for me to grieve more openly.

On numerous occasions when I am in public, I encounter specific reminders of Karla that lead to expressions of grief. Many women in their late twenties with long, blond hair remind me of her, even if their facial features and body shape are not similar to Karla's. That experience ushers in grief. Bird-of-paradise flowers (strelitzia) always remind me of her death; those flowers were featured in her funeral bouquets. I cry more at movies now. Is that because once these emotions emerge in public, I am more sensitive to other kinds of feelings and more comfortable in expressing them?

Karla loved all kinds of music, especially *alternative* music, and when I hear it, in public or in private, I miss her. Just recently, I was in the dentist's office and the piped in music was "Angel" by Sarah McLachlan, the song Kevin used to close his eulogy at her wake. I could no longer talk with the receptionist about scheduling my next appointment.

I have experienced the painful deaths of my parents, a sister, and a brother, also of many other relatives and friends. None of the grief following those deaths does to me what Karla's death does. Ongoing suicide grief, though not persistent anymore, is a permanent part of my emotional DNA. I will die with that loss tattooed on my soul.

Many other suicide survivors and veterans will say the same thing. They, too, grieve involuntarily in public, in the presence of people who are not family. For most of us, it is a new experience to be that emotional, vulnerable, and hurt in public. But the grief is so intense that it overwhelms our lifelong tendency to contain these kinds of fragile feelings. I did not believe this at first, but I do now: It's okay to grieve in public.

Grieving in Private

We also grieve privately, with our family and closest friends. With these loved ones, we usually feel freer to be honest, to share our confusion and anger, depression and guilt, loss and pain. We trust that we are accepted and affirmed, that we can say anything, even what we may not truly believe, but need to say anyway—at least once. We find comfort within this inner circle; it's where we discover sanity in the midst of the emotional disarray following the suicide.

Family dynamics and personalities do not always provide this safe haven, this harbor from the raging seas of grief. When this level of emotional sharing is not present in the family, some people will seek it with a friend or friends, while other grievers will try to bury those feelings and attempt to confront them or ignore them by themselves. It is clearly better to find someone (perhaps a counselor) with whom suicide grievers can identify and express all the grief emotions they experience. Suicide grief support groups and programs also provide a safe environment to work through the pain.

In the final analysis, where we grieve the most is deep within ourselves, privately. It's there in the depth of our being that we confront the loss and the pain with its raw, untamed power. And it's in that deeply personal arena that many of us struggle most fiercely. We simply don't know ourselves accurately enough at this depth and with the intensity needed to face our grief effectively. But it is there, at this deepest level within us, where the suicide grief ultimately resides and rules. When we don't know ourselves at this depth, the grief has free range to do what it wants to do. We can't control it because we have little practice in responding at this level.

The strength of the grief captures our core, squeezes it, and hides it from us, covering it with a heavy, gloomy blanket of sorrow and loss. To release our core, our essence, from the powerful clutches of this grief takes work, honesty, time, and commitment. To throw off the blanket we must have faith that our core is still there, and we must hope that it can be reinstated as the anchor of our being, in place of the grief. If and when we are able to discard that blanket, we travel from survivor to veteran.

Memories

Our loved one who died by suicide also lives in our memories. Memories can both comfort us and torment us, and sometimes the same memories can do both. Memories of a birth, a childhood, an adolescence, of happy birthdays and joyous events, of accomplishments, of struggles overcome and dreams explored, of warm summer nights and playful winter days—memories of the relationship that bound us together and changed us forever.

These happy memories fade when we remember the suicide. Initially, it is hard to remember the good times because the death eclipses the life. The long, cold shadow of suicide freezes the pleasant memories and turns them into hardened dry ice: brittle, inaccessible, untouchable, destructive. The harsh ice captures our joyful memories, encases them in a cocoon of paralyzing grief, and preserves them in an unapproachable block of pain. The suicide regulates the temperature of our memories and keeps them below the freezing point. In the beginning, we cannot melt the ice to feel the warmth of the positive memories.

In time, and with grief work, that terrible ice does begin to melt, and the joyful memories thaw enough to be seen and felt again. They will never be the way they were because they were so brutally frozen, but they will be warm enough to enjoy and temperate enough to be handled. Our loved one rejoins the pantheon of other memories and assumes an honored place in our minds.

We cannot discard the memories. Once we experience our loved ones, we remember them. We may not remember everything about them or everything we did with them or they did without us, but we remember them. We cannot un-live them. Therefore, we cannot un-remember them.

They live in our memories, but it is our choice as to how we remember them. Part of the grief journey is making that choice. How do we want to remember them? We have multiple memories to choose from. Which of those memories, or sets of memories, gets center stage? Ultimately, how we prioritize those memories, which ones have the greatest practical impact on us now, is our responsibility, our choice. Moving them from the frozen tundra of our initial grief to assimilation and the warm sands of a new normal is another way to describe the journey from survivor to veteran. It is a choice. But it is a choice that is earned only after the grief is faced.

Memorials

Memories are internal, inside us. *Memorials* are external, outside us. Most of us need both. The memorials activate the memories, and the memories create the memorials. Together they help us focus on our missing loved ones so we can find a place for them in our lives. Obviously, the memorials and the memories do not replace our loved ones, but they do help us in our dealing with their absence.

The most natural memorial is the grave site. Karla's grave is in Lakeview Memorial Gardens in Fairview Heights, Illinois, in a section labeled Peace. Her grave is among other graves of my family, including my parents, sister, and brother. Fran and I have our plot next to Karla's. There is a large sculpture of the nativity of Jesus about fifty feet to the south of Karla's grave, which is also a short walking distance from the chapel where the final prayers were said and where Father Bill reminded us that Karla was more than her mental illness and suicide. That's where her body is.

And that site is sacred to us. It is a place of memories and longing. It opens doors to the past, to what was and what could have been. It is one spot in the universe that consistently modifies the present with the inexorable truth that death is the final equalizer of life. To know that fact is one thing. To be standing on that site with those graves with familiar names staring back at me is more than a fact; it is a chorus of voices harmonizing the mournful melody of "Amazing Grace" that brings me to my knees weeping while it extols the joy of transformation and new life. It is a place that also predicts the future. Someday I too will die, and most likely, be buried there. My own death is the most absolute truth of my life. Other people will visit my grave, along with the other graves. I will add my voice to the chorus, along with my history. Being there now draws me to being there then.

Karla's grave is where the past, present, and future are most balanced, most aligned in their true perspective. "Live in the present" we are told by wise sages, advice that I respect and try to follow. But the "present" of that grave site *is* the past and the future. It all comes together there, and how we handle the grave says a lot about how we handle the past and the future, as well as the present.

The epitaph on Karla's marker (there are no headstones at Lakeview) repeats a phrase from her version of the Serenity Prayer. It says, "Gently turn my gaze back home, toward simplicity, grace, and gratitude." Home, for Karla, meant our family home, her own home, which was wherever she was able to reside and create her unique space, wherever she experienced simplicity in the midst of enormous emotional complexities, grace in the middle of chaos, and gratitude in place of persistent neediness. Home was also heaven, for she was a deeply spiritual person seeking clarity, authenticity, and love while she opened her arms to her God. Her epitaph reflects her soul.

My guess is that other suicide survivors and veterans have similar feelings regarding the grave sites of their loved one. A visit to the site is often so overwhelming that it is almost impossible to put the emotions into words. We are not accustomed to that much intense emotion, so we can't find the words to express it. But it is valuable to try to find words to describe those visits. When we say it accurately, we are better able to cope with it.

Other Memorials

While the grave site is usually the most prominent memorial, many survivors create other memorials as symbols of their loved one. Here are some examples:

- One person in our suicide survivor support group plants a tree every year in memory of her brother.

- A mother keeps her son's ashes in an urn in an office where she works.

- We have planted some rosebushes and a garden in Karla's

name, and Phil, Fran's nephew, sent us a granite bench with her Serenity Prayer etched in it.

- Ladybugs have unique meaning to us as a remembrance and presence of Karla.

- Many survivors keep pictures and mementoes in special places in their homes. Our support group has a large three-ring binder where survivors include a page representing their loved one.

- Our website offers memorial pages as well.

It is important to create memorials of your loved one in order to preserve his (or her) memory and to help everyone focus on that person's life. Human beings are symbol makers. From religious symbols to cultural, ethnic, and patriotic symbols, we express ourselves through objects that represent us. A picture is worth a thousand words, but a symbol leaves us speechless. It says too much for words, and doesn't need words. To keep your loved one alive in your heart create a symbol of him. While this need for a symbol applies to many people, it is especially valuable when there is a suicide, in order to counteract the unanswerable questions that accompany the suicide.

There may be something that is an obvious symbol of your loved one. If he loved the outdoors, sports, motorcycles, books, animals, outer space, coin collecting, and so forth, a fitting symbol may emerge out of that passion in life. If it isn't obvious what the symbol should be, think about it, consult with others, and create something that will be permanently meaningful. Take your time in deciding upon and developing your symbol; you want it to be relevant and lasting.

Once you have a symbol, use it. Let it speak to you about the positive qualities of your loved one. Let it quiet your mind and inspire your heart. Let it soothe the negative parts of the suicide.

Let it usher you through the pain and into assimilation. Let it help you become a veteran.

Where Are They Now?

Sometimes people come to our support group with one question: Are their loved ones who killed themselves in heaven? Their primary fear is that they may be in hell. If they know they are in heaven, they believe they will be able to deal with the suicide and the grief. But if they are in hell, both the suicide and the grief become much more difficult.

The question "Where are they now?" raises the issue of religious faith. Is there an afterlife, or do we go out of existence when we die? Our answers to these questions have an immediate, profound, and crucial impact on grieving the suicide of a loved one.

My approach here is similar to the position we take with the *Karla Smith Foundation*. We do not endorse any particular religion, denomination, dogma, or theology because we believe that we can support all suicide survivors regardless of their personal beliefs. Suicide grief is difficult for all people, and we want to support them in whatever way we can.

I am a practicing Roman Catholic, but I have kept my personal beliefs out of this section. I simply list some of the possible beliefs associated with an afterlife and what those beliefs may offer to suicide survivors.

1. Some people do not believe in an afterlife, heaven, or hell. They maintain that when we die, regardless of how we die, our lives end. We no longer exist as individuals. There is no soul or spirit that survives the death of the physical body. There is no judgment, no justice, or mercy after death. Regardless of how we lived, virtuously or evilly, we simply cease to exist.

When people with this conviction experience the suicide of a loved one, they can take comfort in the memory of the deceased and the life that their loved one lived, the positive influence he (or she) had on others, and the love that they shared. Their loved one lives on through the impact he had on others, especially if he had children. The life continues through the family, community, or society in general. If the suicide followed years of struggle with mental illness, these survivors may be consoled by the fact that the struggle is now over. Their grief is manageable without a reference to an afterlife.

2. Some people believe in reincarnation. The spirit of the deceased invigorates another being and continues after death, even though the new form this spirit takes does not recall the previous life. This belief insists that a core life form does not go out of existence and that it is ultimately seeking purification and perfection. Suicide is not the optimal way to end a particular life cycle, but it does not negate the cycle. A suicidal life form or spirit may be demoted in the next life but it does continue in its search for perfection.

A suicide griever who believes in reincarnation can join the people in the first example and find consolation in the impact the deceased had on family and friends. But reincarnationists add the possibility of more comfort to their grief knowing that the core life form of their loved one exists in some other way, and will continue to progress until it reaches perfection. The teaching on suicide varies from teacher to teacher. Some condemn it outright, while others are more sympathetic.

3. Many religions profess a belief in a spirit world inhabited by good and evil spirits, angels and demons. Three major world religions, Judaism, Christianity, and Islam all teach about a life after death, in various forms and degrees. The core belief is that a person's life continues in a way that does not

connect with our current life. The person becomes a spirit, living on a different plane, with different modes of being and communicating.

In general, followers of these religions believe that a person who dies by suicide does continue to exist in this spirit world. The nature of that existence is debated, but the fact of that belief offers hope to the survivors.

4. For Christians, even those who no longer participate in a Christian community, the question "Where are they now?" usually comes down to heaven or hell. Other religions have a similar option. Some believers who emphasize God's justice conclude that persons who die by suicide are likely in hell because they have violated a key commandment of God to honor life in all its forms, especially human life. Therefore God's justice demands that they suffer in hell for all eternity.

The giving and taking of human life is in God's hands, and we must not think we can take that control away from God. People who kill themselves are weak sinners who must accept the consequences of their decisions. Survivors can only bow down to God's justice and accept the wisdom of the Almighty, even as they grieve their loved one.

To believers who emphasize the mercy of God, the person who dies by suicide is someone who is "not in his right mind" when he completes the suicide. The God of mercy, as exemplified for Christians by Jesus, accepts them into heaven and nourishes them with forgiveness and love. They exist in this heavenly realm without their pain, mental illness, or impulse which led them to their deaths. These believers find great consolation in the conviction that their loved one is at peace in the loving presence of God.

These four general positions regarding the afterlife are possible ways to respond to the question "Where are they now?" There are variations on all four of them, but I can't think of any other major possibilities. What you believe about this question is crucial to your grief journey. You will have to identify which belief or variation you follow. Whatever your position, incorporate it into your grief journey. You may want to visit with your minister, pastor, rabbi, or a wise person you respect as you consider this question. In any case, to travel from suicide survivor to veteran you will have to walk through one of these doors. The better you are able to process this part of the journey, the better you will be able to assimilate the suicide into your life.

Hope

There are times during the grief journey when it feels like hope is a word without substance, a wish that cannot be fulfilled, a dream that drowns midstream. It feels like there is no end to the loss, guilt, and helplessness.

Even in those most desperate times, there is hope that things will get better. The best way to latch onto that kind of hope is to talk with and be around other people who have also experienced the suicide of a loved one and who have a different and more balanced perspective. We don't normally "think" ourselves into hope. We see it in others; we feel it in them, and we gradually begin to grab some of it for ourselves.

The memorials we create, the memories we cherish, and the beliefs we have about life after death are all pieces to the puzzle that provides a foundation for our hope. We would like to hope that our loved ones will come back, that they would reverse history and not kill themselves, like some time machine in a movie. We want them alive—a natural and intense reaction to their death.

But we know it will never happen. They are gone and we are left behind. That harsh reality is not the basis of our hope. The basis is another reality that stands next to the painful loss, not taking its place, not eliminating, but standing next to it, offering us a basis for a bigger reality, one that includes the harshness of their deaths, but also incorporates more than their death. That accompanying reality is our lives, which are more than their lives, and which encompass more than their deaths. We balance their lives with our lives, and that gives us hope.

When we commemorate their lives in memorials, in symbols outside ourselves, we objectify our feelings and we separate ourselves from them. They are not us. And we can gradually focus on ourselves and our loss instead of them. As we slowly separate, we know that there is more to our lives than their deaths. And that is the beginning of hope.

Questions for Personal Reflection or Group Discussion

1. Does it matter to you where your loved one died? If so, why does it matter? If not, why doesn't it matter?

2. To what extent did the region of the country, the state, city, and neighborhood impact the suicide of your loved one?

3. If your loved one died at home, how has that affected your grief?

4. If your loved one died at a different location, how has that affected your grief?

5. To what extent did you or do you seek help in your grief from a counselor? If you have seen or do see a counselor, what has that experience been like for you? If you did not visit a counselor, how has that decision worked out for you?

6. What has been your experience of grieving in public?

7. What has been your experience of grieving within your family and privately?

8. How do you remember your loved one now? To what extent are your memories pleasant? To what extent are they difficult?

9. What memorials or symbols do you have of your loved one? Describe your feelings as you see or reflect on these memorials.

10. What do you believe about where they are now? Are those beliefs a comfort to you, or are they painful? Or, both?

11. How can you find a basis for hope even while you grieve?

CHAPTER 5

Grieving

Why did they kill themselves? After all the answered, unanswered, and unanswerable questions about *Who*, *What*, *When*, and *Where*, there remains the central, baffling, devastating, and biggest question of all: *Why?* They had options, but they didn't see them or choose them. They thought death was their answer. Their answer remains our question.

In this chapter, I summarize what research tells us about why people die by suicide. I offer the conclusions of the best insights I know about this research. I guide you through the maze of theories surrounding this question, and I point out more questions related to the core issue of why they died.

In the final analysis, however, analysis doesn't satisfy. It is helpful to know the research and how thoughtful people have addressed the question of why some people kill themselves. Their insights help us survivors cope with our grief and give us some words to describe some of our feelings. We learn that we are not alone in our grief and in our search for peace and assimilation, and that not being alone is a great relief. Researchers, writers, and people who share their stories with us and offer us enlightened comfort guide us and move us along on our journey. They help us avoid wrong turns, get around mountains and sheer cliffs, climb walls, and build bridges over raging rivers. But our core grief refuses to be satisfied by analysis and research. We always need more because suicide grief goes much deeper than rational explanations.

So, why even ask the question, *Why?*

I ask it in a book like this because it is a question that all survivors ask themselves. As in all mysteries, it is critical to know where the mystery of suicide begins and ends. If we don't put boundaries around the suicide, the grief will overflow into all areas of our life and swamp us with paralyzing doubt, fear, anger, depression, or guilt. If we don't identify where the mystery of suicide resides, it will reside everywhere. The theories of why people die by suicide help us locate the true mystery—the core *why* of the death. The research doesn't eliminate the ultimate *why*, but it does prevent that *why* from poisoning everything else in our lives. It takes time, commitment, and work to contain the contagion of the *why*, but it does happen. When it happens, a suicide survivor becomes a veteran.

Dr. Thomas Joiner

I begin with what I consider to be the best and most thorough research on the why of suicide. Dr. Thomas Joiner's book *Why People Die by Suicide*[22] is, in my view, the clearest, most comprehensive, best-researched and most compassionate analysis of why people kill themselves. Dr. Joiner is the Robert O. Lawton

---

22   Joiner, *Why People Die by Suicide.*

Distinguished Professor of Psychology at Florida State University in Tallahassee, Florida. His father died by suicide when Dr. Joiner was a graduate student at the University of Texas in 1990. His personal experience, coupled with his academic studies and his career as a professor of psychology, make him an ideal spokesperson for issues related to suicide. When you are finished reading my book, I urge you to read his.

Here is a quote from his book[23] to introduce you to the major components of his theory:

> According to the model described here, serious suicidal behavior requires the desire for death. The desire for death is composed of two psychological states—perceived burdensomeness and failed belongingness. On belongingness, recall the example of the man who left a note in his apartment that said, "I'm going to walk to the bridge. If one person smiles at me on the way, I will not jump." The man jumped to his death. On burdensomeness, recall the study that genuine attempts are often characterized by a desire to make others better off, whereas non-suicidal self-injury is often characterized by a desire to express anger or punish oneself. Examples like these support the direct involvement of failed belongingness and perceived burdensomeness in the desire for death. Either of these two states, in isolation, is not sufficient to instill the desire for death. When these states co-occur, however, the desire for death is produced; if combined with the acquired ability to enact lethal self-injury, the desire for death can lead to a serious suicide attempt or to death by suicide.

Karla fit this model of suicide perfectly. Three factors comprise Dr. Joiner's theory: (1) perceived burdensomeness; (2) failed belongingness, and (3) the acquired ability to enact lethal self-injury.

---

23   Ibid., 136.

Perceived Burdensomeness

There is no question that Karla perceived herself as a burden. It was on Christmas Day, 2002, sitting in our living room on a green plaid love seat, just after she emerged from our guest bedroom, where she spent the previous three hours in somber depression, that she told us, "I am a burden to you and to the whole universe. I am not worth the chemicals that make up my body." All our efforts to convince her otherwise, all our gentle testimonies that we loved her and that we would be there for her regardless of where her illness took her, all our reminders of happier times in the past, all our descriptions of her wonderful qualities—none of it really helped. She smiled weakly and knew what we were trying to do, and we hugged, but nothing penetrated the steel chamber that the depression had built in her heart. It was one of the saddest moments of my life. Three weeks later, she shot herself.

That wasn't the first time she spoke of her burdensomeness. On other occasions, with previous depressions, she said similar things. But she wasn't always that gloomy. When she was balanced, before her need for medication, and during her sometimes lengthy periods of stability, she was a cheerful, optimistic, exuberant, and engaging person. Her "normal" state was upbeat and positive, adventuresome, fearless, and delighting in relationships and ideas. She did not have a melancholy bone in her beautiful body or a defeatist thought in her lively mind. Suicide was inconceivable to her and to anyone who knew her. Until the depression.

My guess is that many other suicide survivors and veterans have similar stories to tell of their loved ones. Details certainly vary and personalities differ, but the core experience of trying to convince potential suiciders that they are not the burden they say they are remains the same. That is why the burdensomeness that Dr. Joiner describes is perceived, not real. Our loved ones think they are more of a burden than they really are. They also conclude that we would be better off without them, regardless of what we say. Their mental illness creates this thinking, and their desperate feelings of despair follow their thinking. We try to change their minds, but the depression knows better. We are left with a sense of powerlessness and weary frustration. And they believe they remain a liability to our lives and to all of life.

On the other hand, and to be honest, there *is* a burden that does come with depression and other forms of mental illness. Not all of it is perception. There is a genuine affliction for the person who suffers from it and for those of us who love that person. Coping with Karla's bipolar disorder was not easy, and it pushed us to the edge of our ability to relate to her, to know how to love and support her, to keep her safe, and to help her deal with life and other people. After the first symptoms of her illness emerged, we gave more time and energy to her and her problems than we did to her twin brother Kevin and his life. She was in greater need, and we had no path to follow in supporting her. She was a greater weight to carry emotionally, and it wore us down. And we often worried that we might be neglecting Kevin to some extent because we were focused so much on Karla. Kevin, too, felt her weight as he went to great lengths to help his twin sister. In other words, her illness was a true burden not only to herself but to all of us.

Many families disengage from a family member with a mental illness because of this kind of burden. Too many bridges have been crossed; too many family fights have been fought; too many relationships are damaged; too many jobs have been lost. The affliction of mental illness has casualties in multiple directions, and some of them last till death. Homelessness or prison, and being without support from disheartened family members is the fate of too many people with a mental illness

Other members in our support group also report the burdens that accompanied the mental illness of their loved ones. Their testimony is similar to ours. As we grieve, we don't want to focus on this burdensomeness because it feels like we are blaming someone who died by suicide and because we feel guilty that we didn't accept the challenge of supporting them. We let them down. Naming this guilt and working through it is one of the tasks of suicide grief. We would rather have our loved ones alive, even with the difficulties their lives brought us, than to have them die the way they did. But for many of us, there was a level of true burden coping with their mental illness.

Some members of our group grieve the suicide of a loved one who had no diagnosed mental illness or obvious signs of a mental illness. It may be that the illness was present but not diagnosed. But in some situations, the suicide appears to be an impulse, sometimes connected with alcohol or drugs and sometimes not. There was no previous experience of unusual burdensomeness. At times, there was a breakup of a relationship coupled with other stressful factors, but nothing that clearly adds up to suicide, in our view. But obviously, from the perspective of the one who died, something happened that made suicide an attractive alternative to life. It is reasonable to assume, as Dr. Joiner does, that at the time of their deaths they perceived themselves to be a burden. Whatever it was that drove them to that deadly moment, they likely felt that they and some other people would be better off if they died. This presumption is not an effort to "force" their deaths into Dr. Joiner's theory; it is a sensible interpretation of the suicidal motives that remain a mystery but which cry out for some realistic explanation of an essentially mindless act.

The perceived burdensomeness factor, it seems, is a crucial and universal element needed to describe the psychological pain that overwhelms the judgment of someone who seriously attempts suicide.

Failed Belongingness

We are made to belong. We start with our mothers, and branch out to our fathers and other close family members, eventually including friends and acquaintances. Perhaps more accurately, as infants and toddlers, they belong to us. We need others to stay alive until we become self-sufficient enough to take care of ourselves. Even then, we need others throughout life for social, emotional, economic, physical, spiritual and intellectual support.

But needing others is not the same as feeling connected. I have felt that I didn't belong during some cocktail parties, or at meetings I had no interest in, or in a job I was not suited for. When that feeling, which I assume most of us have experienced, expands to all of life, one of Dr. Joiner's necessary elements for suicide is in place.[24]

Karla belonged to numerous groups and had multiple personal relationships. Like most of us, she navigated through these groups and relationships relatively successfully. But once again like most of us, she felt left out at various points in life. How did her feelings of being left out expand to the sense of failed belongingness that Dr. Joiner identifies as a component of a serious suicide attempt?

Karla attempted suicide three times prior to her completed suicide. Her first attempt was during her initial depression, when she was nineteen. She was living at home and took the pills in our medicine cabinet, called us at work to tell us good-bye, and wrote in lipstick on our bathroom mirror, "I am no longer a poet. I lost all my words." Fortunately, Fran got there in time to get her to a hospital where they pumped her stomach.

Seven years later, in the suicide note which she wrote when she tried to convince Lonnie to agree to a murder-suicide pact, she wrote that she could speak no more and that she would spend

---

24   Ibid., 117–134.

the rest of her life in a catatonic silence. Since spoken and written words were so important to her, they symbolized life for her. On the flip side, not speaking and losing her words symbolized death, not belonging anymore. When she couldn't speak or write, it was her way of saying that she couldn't live. Literally.

Failed belongingness is extremely difficult for suicide grievers. It leaves us feeling like we failed our loved ones. If they belonged to anyone, they belonged to us who loved them. Why didn't they feel that love and support? Didn't we express it often enough, clearly enough, in ways that led them to know they could count on us? Did we fail them? If they remembered those decades of love, surely they would have known that they belonged in our hearts and lives, right? They had to know we loved them, didn't they?

Karla's suicide tells me that none of this love was strong enough to counteract her practiced depression. During that final month before she died, she became convinced that she didn't belong to us, or to anyone. The isolation of her illness was complete. She was pregnant at the time of her death; the child was conceived while she was in a manic, psychotic period. We suspect that the father was a graduate student (name unknown to us) whom she had recently met and who may not even know he was a father.

In effect, the father did not belong emotionally either to Karla or to the growing baby. She told us of the pregnancy at Christmas, and we supported her and agreed with her plan to have the baby adopted. She seemed convinced of that approach, and given the circumstances and her emotional state, it seemed the wisest course to us also. But I wonder now if the adoption also contributed to her failed belongingness. She didn't even "belong" to her own baby. Not only did she not have a husband, she was giving up her baby as well.

She was also under-medicated because of her pregnancy. In the beginning of December 2002, a doctor reduced her antidepressant dosage to a minimum to avoid any possible injury to her fetus. Karla agreed to this lower dosage plan, but it was clearly not enough to fight off the depression. When Fran got her to a treatment center on New Year's Eve in a catatonic state, they immediately increased her dosage. Ten days later, on a Friday, they released her against our wishes. She died the following Monday.

She had always talked longingly of her eventual family—of having a loving husband and lots of kids. Her reality undermined that expectation. She didn't belong to her own dream.

Was this line of thinking the final reality that pulled the trigger on January 13, 2003? Many people have expectations and dreams that are blocked by a disappointing reality, and most of these people don't kill themselves. But with Karla, at this point, the combination of her perceived burdensomeness, failed belongingness, and previous suicide attempts coalesced into the desire and ability to take her own life. From her perspective, the pregnancy and adoption plan closed off her last chance to belong. This observation, though not answering the ultimate question of *why*, does offer a plausible description of her mind as she died. It's a guess, but a reasonable guess.

While people in our support group haven't used this terminology of failed or thwarted connectedness, they recognize the concept when I mention it. Some of them use phrases like "He seemed remote," or "She was clearly depressed." Other members say that they didn't notice any change and were surprised and shocked by the suicide. Still others, whose loved one died at a distance and whom they hadn't seen or talked with for a while, don't know the state of mind of their loved one and are haunted by that unknown. They can only speculate.

Our last phone conversation with Karla was the Sunday night before she died. We had talked with her earlier that day, and she mentioned that she had thrown up, probably due to the pregnancy. We called her back to say that she probably lost her medication with her nausea, and that she should call her doctor about her antidepressant. She agreed to do that the next day. Had she already decided that she would kill herself when we talked with her? We will never know.

Does Dr. Joiner's theory of perceived burdensomeness, failed belongingness, and acquired ability to inflict self-injury fit all situations? I suspect that it does, even though there are many unknowns and variations that surround suicide. I suggest that when you ask the *why* question, think about these three factors, and see if they offer some explanation of the death of your loved one. It is the closest I can come to answering that question about Karla.

The Acquired Ability to Enact Lethal Self-Injury

The third component of Dr. Joiner's theory about why people die by suicide is that it takes practice to arrive at a level of self-injury sufficient to kill yourself. For many suicides this progression from less dangerous behavior to most dangerous suicidal attempts is fairly easy to trace. The innate desire to live, to self-preserve, is so deeply ingrained in the human psyche (and, it seems, in most life forms) that it takes considerable effort and practice to counteract this desire. To die by suicide people need more than perceived burdensomeness and failed belongingness. They need to *want* to die. An attitude of wanting to die is not easy to come by, and seriously attempting suicide is even harder.

So, how do thirty-eight thousand people in the United States and one million people worldwide complete suicide each year? They gradually build up to it through acts of self-injury. They become accustomed to the pain associated with self-injury, or they engage in risky behavior that conditions them to the higher risk of suicide, or they become comfortable with impulsive thinking and acting to the extent that they don't consider consequences. In other words, they build up to a suicide attempt.

This deadly progression is very clear with Karla. She was always adventuresome: the only one in the family who wanted to go on the roller-coaster, the parachute drop, leap into the deep end of the pool when she was child, travel to Europe in college without much of a plan, stop in a pub in the Netherlands because it was there, experiment with drugs in high school just to see what it was like, befriend a stripper in San Antonio while a freshman in college. Many people have done similar and riskier things without developing suicidal tendencies, but with Karla, it likely set the stage for her suicide.

Dr. Joiner's theory, I now know, would red flag this pattern of behavior. Karla's style of life, at least this adventuresome part of it, could have been an indicator that she was building up a potential for suicide, not by itself but in combination with the eventual perceived burdensomeness and failed belongingness. Once she attempted suicide the first time, during her initial onslaught of clinical depression, the possibility of a future completed suicide increased dramatically. Her subsequent attempts reinforced her ability to inflict fatal self-injury. By then, I was aware of the danger and lived every day in the shadow of that lethal possibility.

But according to Dr. Joiner's theory, she was on that trajectory for a long time. It wasn't inevitable or predetermined, but it was pointed in the direction of potential suicide. She was familiar with risky behavior; she was willing to experiment with life; she enjoyed the thrill of the unknown; she loved the challenge of new thinking; she pushed the boundaries in relationships and excitement. And then she had bipolar disorder.

I know this now. I didn't know it then. I wish I had.

This progression that I can now trace with Karla may or may not be evident in other suicides. With some members of our support group, a similar pattern with their loved one can be seen. With other members, particularly those who lost loved ones who had no diagnosed mental illness or who died seemingly by an impulsive single act, it is less clear how Dr. Joiner's theory responds to the *why* question. But I still believe that even in these situations his approach provides the best framework for a reasonable response, and while nothing completely tells us why they die by suicide, his research and conclusions get us as close as we can get. Perceived burdensomeness, failed belongingness, and the acquired ability to inflict lethal self-injury, when combined, most likely describe critical dimensions of the mind of people who seriously attempt or complete suicide. Once again, I encourage you to read Joiner's book.

Other Approaches

Dr. Joiner's book goes into some detail regarding other theories on why people die by suicide. He does so to acknowledge their work and his dependence on some of their conclusions and methods. But he also points out where his theory differs from theirs and where his analysis goes further. Here I mention just a few of these other researchers, in case you want to study them yourself, and to verify that other professionals, though not enough of them, have addressed suicide from an academic perspective.

- Émile Durkheim, *Le Suicide: Etude de socologie* (Paris: F. Alcan), 1897.

  English translation by John A. Spaulding and George Simpson, *Suicide: A Study in Sociology* (The Free Press, Simon & Schuster Inc., New York), 1951.

  Durkheim's theory emphasized the role of society in an individual's suicide. No other significant theories emerged until the latter half of the twentieth century.

- Edwin Schneidman, *The Suicidal Mind* (Oxford University Press, New York), 1996.

  This and Schneidman's other books on suicide provide a base for modern theories on suicide. Schneidman coined the word *psychache* to describe the psychological cause of suicide. He maintained that psychache originates in blocked emotional needs. Joiner identifies and gives names to these frustrated needs: burdensomeness and belongingness. Schneidman also identifies the critical role of lethality in his understanding of suicide.

- Aaron T. Beck and colleagues, *Relationship between hopelessness and ultimate suicide: A replication with psychiatric outpatients* (American Journal of Psychiatry), 1990, 190– 105.

  Hopelessness is the central factor in this theory of suicide.

Other researchers have worked on the problem as well. (Roy Baumeister[25] and Marsha Linehan[26] are two more that Joiner comments on.) I mention them in this book to assure you that serious, intelligent, competent professionals are committed to clarifying the answer to that most difficult question of *why* our loved ones took their lives. We are not alone in struggling with this devastating issue. Not only are there other survivors and veterans to walk with us and support us in our grief, but qualified and dedicated researchers are working hard to offer us the best possible insights into the perplexing question of why someone could and would overcome the powerful, innate drive for self-preservation to kill himself. It is comforting to know that this

---

25   Baumeister, R.F. & Leary, M.R. (1995) The need to belong: Desire for interpersonal attachments as a fundamental human motivation. *Psychological Review, 117,* 497-529

26   Linehan, M.M. (1993) *Cognitive-behavioral Treatment of Borderline Personality Disorder* New York:Guilford Press

research takes place, and the findings of these experts give us some words and understanding as we grieve.

In my view, Dr. Joiner offers the best of that helpful research.

Suicide Grieving—The *Why* Question

Trying to answer the *why* question is one thing; grieving the *why* question is something else. Regardless of how well we can answer this question intellectually, suicide grievers struggle with it emotionally as soon as we hear about the suicide. Why? The news rips through our hearts and devours our psyche like an EF5 tornado before it even reaches our mind. We ask the question before we are capable of responding to it, and the question keeps repeating itself even though we know we can't answer it.

The grief that chases the *why* question carries with it a special kind of agony. Other deaths are also painful and long-lasting. My father died in a hospital from pneumonia following a series of small strokes at age seventy-seven. A sister (fifty-two) and my brother (sixty-seven) both died from cancer. My mother, in a fetal position, died slowly of Alzheimer's at age ninety-two after ten years of gradually losing the graciousness, strength, and warmth that marked her life. All of these family deaths left a wake of grief that took time and emotional work to assimilate into my ongoing life. I am who I am in many ways because of them, and I am changed permanently because of their lives and deaths. Grieving them prepared me somewhat for grieving Karla. But her suicide was not a more intense form of the same kind of grief. Karla's death was a different kind of grief.

The *why* question exposes that difference. All other deaths have a clear cause. Some other deaths may raise some questions: How did the fatal accident happen? What caused the cancer or heart disease? Could we have prevented the death? Perhaps a different doctor or an experimental treatment? Should we have allowed them to discontinue the feeding tubes? Significant questions, no doubt. But none of them go to the heart of the death. In all of them, we know the basic circumstances and cause of the death.

But when there is a suicide, the core question of why they died remains open, even when we know immediately a mental illness was involved. We have not yet arrived at the point of saying "She died of depression" in the same way we can say "He died of cancer." There is still too much stigma and too much presumed choice in dying by suicide. As a result, our suicide grief is qualitatively different from grieving other deaths.

Theories like Dr. Joiner's are extremely helpful as we try to get a handle on grieving the *why* question. But we study and still grieve. And we grieve a lot and a long time before we can focus enough to begin to study why people take their lives. Many grievers are unaccustomed to reading research books on anything, so they will most likely not research the cause of suicide either. Other grievers need to read and search for answers, but do it too fast and get lost in all the written words and their own scrambled emotions. Some suicide grievers are so overwhelmed initially that they can't "think straight."

But all grievers ask why their loved ones died by suicide. When they ask, they need short responses at first, until they are able to handle longer comments. Dr. Joiner provides the longer answers, and support groups like ours, along with grief counselors of all kinds, offer the short answers and point to the longer explanations. Throughout this process, most grievers keep asking why.

Iris Bolton reminds us that sometimes we ask the *why* question until we no longer need to ask it.[27] As suicide survivors progress to suicide veterans, the need to know why seems to lessen. We get

---

27   Iris Bolton with Curtis Mitchell, *My Son…My Son,* Bolton Press, Atlanta, 1983

partial answers along the way and then conclude and accept that there may never be a final, totally conclusive explanation of why our loved one died. And that reality is enough for us to assimilate the suicide into our lives and continue to live with hope and happiness. We live with the question. We adjust, we remember, we honor, we miss, we wonder what if, we cry, but we live. We assimilate and we are at peace, not necessarily with the suicide but with ourselves.

Impulsivity

Is suicide impulsive? I ask this question in particular because a number of people in our support group grieve the suicide of a loved one who had no known previous history of mental illness and who gave no indication that they were suicidal. I see these friends struggle with this part of their grief, and I suspect that other survivors also have no easy answer to this question.

Even with Karla, who was clearly and gravely depressed at the time of her death, I ask myself some impulse-related questions. Did she have her death all planned out? Was she simply looking for an opportunity and means to die, and it presented itself when Lonnie left his apartment and she found his rifle? Did she know when she went there that Monday morning that she would die that day? Or did she just happen to find the gun and decide then and there to shoot herself—impulsively? If she hadn't found the gun and then decided to use it, would she still be alive today? How hard was it to make that final "decision" to pull the trigger? Was it a decision at all? Or did her depression operate on its own and propel her to take the opportunity when it appeared, fulfilling a determination to die made much earlier than that morning?

If those questions occur to me in the clear face of Karla's bipolar depression, similar but even more intense questions emerge when there is no obvious indication of mental illness. Statistics say that between 90 and 95 percent of people who die by suicide have a diagnosable mental illness at the time of death. What about the 5 to 10 percent of those who do not fit that statistic? Are they impulse deaths? If so, why would they go to that extreme? Finally, as in the case of my questions about Karla, to what extent is impulsiveness a part of many other suicides?

While research indicates that impulsivity is a risk factor for suicide, it is less clear how an impulse directly impacts a particular suicide. It seems improbable that a single impulse could overcome the strong, innate drive to preserve our own lives. Joiner suggests that impulsivity has an indirect effect on a suicide, that a pattern of impulsive behavior preconditions someone to hurt himself permanently by suicide.[28] As a result, Joiner speculates, a "spur-of-the-moment" suicide does not happen. He would argue that you could look at previous behavior and see a pattern of risky, impulsive behavior that leads someone to gradually become accustomed to self-injury to such an extent that suicide is not that surprising. When this accumulated behavior is joined with perceived burdensomeness and failed belongingness, the conditions for a serious suicide attempt are present.

Is this analysis comforting to those grievers who struggle with the impulsiveness of their loved one who completed suicide? I hope so.

Alcohol and Drugs

Alcohol and abusive, nonmedical drugs also enter into the response about why people die by suicide, as I mentioned in chapter 1. It is commonly known that alcohol and drugs are, at times, used by some people with mental illness to counteract the impact of their illness. They self-medicate in an effort to erase the

---

28   Ibid., 184–188.

symptoms of the illness. It doesn't help, and in fact, alcohol and drugs are usually even more disastrous in situations dealing with mental illness. Alcohol and drugs dismantle legitimate mental health treatment approaches and make matters worse by adding another major obstacle to the road to recovery. Addictions often follow. The combination of mental illness with alcohol or drugs dramatically increases the possibility of suicide. Treatment for people with all three problems becomes more complicated, and among them the rate of suicide goes way up.

When people with alcohol or drug addictions die by suicide, the grievers must deal with these addictions as factors in the death. Sometimes alcohol or drugs are part of the suicide even if there is no addiction. These substances can lower inhibitions, interfere with judgment, encourage impulsivity, increase depression, and lead to suicide.

These suicide grievers have to deal with the death as well as all the emotions and reactions to the alcohol and drug use. They ask, "Could I have prevented the substance abuse and therefore stopped the suicide?" The abuse of alcohol and drugs is usually long-standing, but even if it was a single, fatal event, could I have prevented it? These are more questions that often go unanswered, which prolong and complicate the grief journey of suicide survivors.

Who Is to Blame?

When a loved one dies by suicide, the ultimate *why* question often comes down to: Who is to blame for this death? It is a natural enough question since we tend to seek a cause for what happens. From three-year-olds asking *why* about everything and not being satisfied about any of the answers they get to ninety-year-olds still wondering why we do the things we do, we look to find the reasons for things. Therefore, in a case of suicide it is predictable and normal to search for someone or something to blame for the death.

There are a variety of choices for fault in a suicide. Survivors can blame themselves for not preventing the suicide: If only I had been there. If only I had seen the warning signs more clearly. If only I had changed something. If only I had stayed with him (or her) more closely. If only we had not had an argument. If only … The *if onlys* are as varied as the suicides. We could all find some basis for blaming ourselves if we wanted to.

We could blame other people for the suicide. There may have been a broken relationship or someone who was mean to our loved one, and this destructive relationship was the proximate cause of the death.

We could blame the doctors and mental health care professionals for not providing proper treatment or right meds or effective counseling. This is an area that I needed to get into perspective because I did blame the treatment center for releasing Karla too early, before she was strong enough to resist the suicide temptation. I know she must have fooled them into believing that she was stable enough to be released, but they should have known better. As we found out later, a judge signed off on her release, a judge who didn't know her except for the report the staff of the center presented. For a long time I blamed them, but eventually I cooled off enough to view their decision to release her from another perspective. They did the best they knew what to do at the time, for whatever reasons they had. In any case, continuing to blame those involved isn't going to bring my daughter back to me. We have some evidence that the facility adjusted their policy to some degree, so perhaps they have not made that mistake again. Other suicide grievers have similar stories.

We could also blame the brain disorder, the illness, or the genetic disposition, and that blame may very well be justified. But is that blame any different than blaming cancer for all the deaths it causes? It is a waste of emotional energy to blame an illness; we have complex but vulnerable bodies to begin with, and the brain is the most complex organ we have. It is no wonder that it doesn't always function correctly. There are so many chemicals and minute parts of the brain that we are still searching for the answers to how it all works, let alone knowing how to fix parts that don't work properly. But if we need something to blame, the illness itself, the brain disorder, the depression is a legitimate target of our anger and frustration.

Depending on the kind of faith we profess, we may find ourselves blaming God for the suicide. If we believe that God controls our lives in considerable detail, then God would be involved in this death. Or if we believe in the explicit activity of the devil, we may conclude that the devil caused the mental illness and the suicide. In any case, either the Deity or the Evil One caused the suicide.

We could blame some external event that created the circumstances which contributed to the death: perhaps an economic crisis; loss of reputation; loss of a job, the death of a spouse, family member, or friend; or events in society at large.

We could blame our loved ones who died by suicide. They are not to blame for having depression or some other form of mental illness but they were responsible, at least to some degree, for their recovery, for managing their illness. They couldn't or wouldn't do what they needed to do to keep the worst of the illness at bay, so it was their fault that they died.

So, we have many choices for finding someone or something to blame. It is natural that we try to find fault somewhere when we ask the *why* question. And in any given suicide, one or more of the categories above may fit. We could cast blame for years.

But what is the point? Blame gives us a target, even if it is ourselves, to focus our anger on. We can release pent-up, negative feelings by accusing someone of causing, or partially causing, the suicide of our loved one. There may even be truth in some of our accusations. But once we release those emotions by expressing them, they quickly build up, and the cycle of blame begins again—and again, and again! The problem is that blaming doesn't help us grieve, become suicide veterans, or assimilate the death into our lives. Finding fault only deepens our negative feelings, and distracts us from our grief journey.

How do we let go of the urge to blame? Forgiveness and gratitude lead to peace and assimilation. We learn to forgive our loved one, and anyone else we tend to condemn for the suicide. We learn forgiveness by practicing forgiveness, beginning with smaller pieces, until there is nothing and no one left to forgive. Talk about the blame to trusted family members and friends or to a counselor. Talk about it until you don't have to talk about it anymore. If possible, tell people you forgive them. No one wanted your loved one to die by suicide. If necessary, write a letter to your loved one, saying that you forgive him. Keep the letter for future reading. He had an illness and died. Depression—mental illness—can be lethal, like cancer, diabetes, or heart disease. No one is to blame. It is one of the many ways we die. The illness killed your loved one.

Gratitude also helps us move out of the blame game. There are things about your loved one that you can be thankful for. Remember them. Talk about them. We had Karla for twenty-six years, and while there were clearly some very difficult times and events during her life, there were also some wonderful times and events. She was a unique, lovely person, and I need to be grateful for her because that, too, is a genuine part of our personal history. Her death does not erase her life. Learn to be thankful.

The reward for replacing blame with forgiveness and gratitude is peace and assimilation. Peace means an untroubled heart, and assimilation means I can continue on in life with a positive outlook and a smile on my soul. That's the outcome we all deserve.

Hope

Hope is a noun and a verb. As a noun, *hope* is the conviction that what we want will happen. Events will turn out as we want them to; our expectations will be fulfilled. As a verb, *hope* means to look forward with confidence, trusting that our desired outcome will take place. In this section, I focus on hope as a verb, as an action.

When we start asking the *why* question immediately on hearing about the suicide, we cannot hope because we don't know what to hope for, and our feelings of shock, loss, and grief consume us. In time, there is room for hoping. Our hope is to feel better, to rediscover how to be happy again, to include the suicide into our life but not have the suicide determine our life. But we know that kind of life is not possible until we deal with the questions this book raises. The *Who, What, When, Where,* and *Why* questions are all swirling around within us, unorganized, randomly bumping into each other, and complicating our ability to answer them or even to ask them without confusion.

The intent of this book is to walk with you as you pose those questions. As you find some answers, accept that some questions have no answers, and accept that you are now comfortable enough with the answers you have that you are able to assimilate the suicide into your life. As such, this book was an act of hoping, of seeing a better future for you, and a tool to move you into a new way of viewing the suicide and yourself.

Since *hope* here is a verb, this journey to assimilation as a suicide veteran is never finished. We never completely arrive. But the road is smoother, the views are prettier, the weather is pleasanter, our traveling companions are more relaxed and enjoying the trip with us, and there is a lovely valley up ahead with a diner that features homemade cooking with pie for desert. We will have to get back into the car again because the journey is not over, but we have a foundation for hoping that the continuing trip will be okay. There will be some bumpy roads, the view may become monotonous, and a storm may slow us down, but we know we will make it through to another lovely valley and another delightful diner. We know that, because we have hope as a permanent part of our heart, right next to the memory of our loved one who died by suicide.

Questions for Personal Reflection or Group Discussion

1. Do you agree that the ultimate answer to the *why* question remains a mystery? Explain your answer.

2. What are the three components of Dr. Joiner's theory about why people die by suicide?

3. Describe *perceived burdensomeness* in your own words. To what extent did your loved one experience this burdensomeness? How did he (or she) express this sense of burden on others?

4. Describe *failed belongingness* in your own words. To what extent, did your loved one experience this failed belongingness? How did he express this failure?

5. Describe the *acquired ability to enact lethal self-injury* in your own words. To what extent did your loved one experience this acquired ability? How did he demonstrate that he had this ability?

6. How does the grief following other deaths of your loved ones compare with the grief of the suicide death?

7. To what extent was *impulsivity* a factor in the suicide of your loved one? How has this factor affected your grief?

8. To what extent was alcohol or drugs a factor in the suicide of your loved one? How has this factor affected your grief?

9. Were there other major factors not included in this book that influenced the suicide of your loved one? If so, what are those factors, and how do they affect your grief?

10. Whom do you tend to blame for the suicide? How well do you handle this blame? How do you see lowering or eliminating this feeling of blame?

11. What are you hoping for as you grieve the suicide? To what extent do you believe you will achieve the goal of that hope? What or who will help you become a suicide veteran?

Acknowledgments

Many people are part of this book. Family, friends, support group members, people I met at conferences, people on committees, authors I have read, phone calls, even one-time conversations all have some impact on this book because they have some impact on me. Thank you.

From this general group, I am particularly grateful to:

Father Charles Rubey, who wrote the Foreword to this book, and who is a longtime friend and the founder and director of LOSS (Loving Outreach to Survivors of Suicide), a Chicago-based suicide survivor program that has comforted thousands of grievers for over thirty years. I thank him for his personal support, wisdom, and professional guidance as we launched the Karla Smith Foundation.

Our KSF support group for anyone who lost a loved one to suicide. We meet on the second and fourth Thursday of each month to encourage each other, learn, cry, seek, and find some hope, and to speak our hearts and minds openly, without judgment. The group lives in these pages. Thank you for your honesty, strength, sincerity, and insights along with your grief and pain.

The staff at iUniverse for their commitment and expertise in publishing this book.

My immediate family: my wife, Fran, son, Kevin, and daughter-in-law, Emily. They make up the personal and professional framework in which I live and work, and their encouragement throughout the development of this book made it possible for me to continue and complete this project. I love all of you, each specifically and uniquely, but as a family as well.

Bibliography

Baugher, Bob, PhD, and Jack Jordan, PhD. *After Suicide Loss: Coping with Your Grief.* Newcastle, WA: Bob Baugher, 2002.

Bolton, Iris, with Curtis Mitchell. *My Son ... My Son: A Guide to Healing after Death, Loss, or Suicide.* Atlanta: Bolton Press, 1983.

Cobain, Beverly and Larch, Jean. *Dying to be Free: A Healing Guide for Families after a Suicide.* Center City, MN: Hazelden Foundation, 2006

Durkheim, Émile. *Suicide.* New York: The Free Press, Simon & Schuster Inc., 1951.

Jamison, Kay Redfield. *An Unquiet Mind.* New York: Vintage Books, Random House Inc., 1995.

———. *Night Falls Fast: Understanding Suicide.* New York: Vintage Books, Random House Inc., 1999.

Joiner, Thomas. *Why People Die by Suicide.* Cambridge, MA: Harvard University Press, 2005.

Joiner, Thomas. *Myths About Suicide.* Cambridge, MA: Harvard University Press, 2010

Lukas, Christopher and Seiden, Henry. *Silent Grief: Living in the Wake of Suicide.* Philadelphia, PA: Jessica Kingsley Publishers, 2007

Marcus, Eric. *Why Suicide: Questions and Answers about Suicide, Suicide Prevention, and Coping with the Suicide of Someone You Know.* New York: HarperCollins, 2010

Schneidman, Edwin S. *The Suicidal Mind.* New York: Oxford University Press, 1996.

Smith, Tom. *The Tattered Tapestry: A Family's Search for Peace with Bipolar Disorder.* Indianapolis, IN: iUniverse, 2005

Smith, Tom. *A Balanced Life, 9 Strategies for Coping with the Mental Health Problems of a Loved One.* Center City, MN: Hazelden, 2008

Wolfelt, Alan D., PhD. *Understanding Your Suicide Grief.* Collins: Companion Press, Col, 2009.

Wrobleski, Adina. *Suicide: Survivors, A Guide for Those Left Behind.* Minneapolis: Afterwords, 1994.

Resources

The organizations and websites I mention here are the ones that I believe will be the most helpful for anyone who wishes to pursue the topic of suicide grief further. If anyone wishes to delve deeper into any of the themes related to suicide, suicide prevention, and suicide grief, I suggest you google the theme and search the web.

Organizations and Websites:

American Association of Suicidology
5221 Wisconsin Avenue, NW
Washington, DC 20015
Phone: (202) 237-2280
Fax: (202) 237-2282
www.suicidology.org

American Foundation for Suicide Prevention
120 Wall Street, 29th Floor
New York, NY 10005
(212) 363-6237
www.afsp.org

Karla Smith Foundation
7 Eagle Center, Suite 2H
O'Fallon, IL 62269
www.KarlaSmithFoundation.org

To find a support group for anyone who lost a loved one to suicide:
http://www.afsp.org/index.cfm?fuseaction=home.
viewPage&page_id=FEE4D90C-A27B-456E-
36DDF23261B4378D

Centers for Disease Control and Prevention
1600 Clifton Road
Atlanta, GA 30333
800-CDC-INFO (800-232-4636)
http://www.cdc.gov/violenceprevention/suicide/

Alliance of Hope for Suicide Survivors
http://www.allianceofhope.org/alliance-of-hope-for-suic/
welcome.html

National Institute of Mental Health
6001 Executive Boulevard
Rockville, MD 20852

LOSS (Loving Outreach to Survivors of Suicide)
721 N. LaSalle Street
Chicago, IL 60654
Main line: (312) 655-7283
http://www.catholiccharities.net/loss

Survivors of Suicide
http://www.survivorsofsuicide.com/resource_links.shtml